keyboard
facts

the essential reference guide for keyboard players

Thunder Bay Press

An imprint of the Advantage Publishers Group
5880 Oberlin Drive, San Diego, CA 92121
www.thunderbaybooks.com

All notifications of errors or omissions should be addressed to Thunder
Bay Press, Editorial Department, at the above address. All other
correspondence (author inquiries, permissions) concerning the content
of this book should be addressed to Outline Press (Book Publishers) Ltd,
2a Union Court, 20-22 Union Road, London SW4 6JP, England.

ISBN-13: 978-1-59223-877-4
ISBN-10: 1-59223-877-7

1 2 3 4 5 12 11 10 09 08

Origination and print by Colorprint (Hong Kong)

Editor: **John Morrish**
Design: **Paul Cooper Design; Johnathan Elliott, Mental Block;**
       Balley Design Limited

Contents

1 the players

Fats Waller

Alongside Art Tatum and Count Basie, Thomas Wright "Fats" Waller was one of the most notable jazz pianists of the early 20th century. He helped to popularize the semi-improvised "stride" piano style, which he picked up from fellow New Yorker James P. Johnson, author of the 1923 hit "Charleston." A variant of ragtime, stride piano is characterized by pulse-like playing—often with a tenth interval on the first and third beats—with the left hand and contrapuntal riffs and melodies with the right.

Born in 1904, Waller studied with Johnson as a teenager before making his first recording at the age of 18. In his twenties he worked as an accompanist at silent-movie theaters in and around New York before finding fame in his own right. As well as being one of the era's finest pianists, Waller was also a prolific songwriter. Among the many songs he wrote during the 20s and 30s are "Ain't Misbehavin'" and "Honeysuckle Waltz." As his success grew he toured internationally, appeared in movies, and wrote a Broadway show, *Hot Chocolates*.

Waller died in 1943 at the age of 39, but remains a highly regarded figure. A Broadway musical based around his songs, *Ain't Misbehavin'*, opened in 1978, a year after his music was featured prominently in the movie *Eraserhead*. Much of the 2008 movie *Be Kind Rewind*, meanwhile, concerns the efforts of a young video-store clerk to make a fictionalized movie about Waller's life. TJS

▲ **Fats Waller**
A prolific songwriter and fine pianist

Art Tatum

Art Tatum was one of the most imaginative and technically gifted pianists of the 20th century; indeed, the esteemed jazz critic Leonard Feather has called him "the greatest soloist in jazz history, regardless of instrument."

Born in 1909 in Toledo, Ohio, Tatum had very poor vision, being blind in one eye and only partially sighted in the other. He had some training at the city's school of music, where he learned to read notation, using glasses and Braille, but was for the most part self-taught, learning from piano rolls, radio, and records. His first professional performances came in 1926 and he first appeared on radio in 1929; recordings followed, in 1933, after he had moved to New York as accompanist for the singer Adelaide Hall.

In the beginning Tatum played in the stride style made famous by Fats Waller, but soon moved beyond that into sophisticated and exuberant rhythmic and harmonic recreations of popular tunes, for instance "Tea For Two" and "Tiger Rag." His reharmonizations, particularly, were well ahead of their time, making him a key influence on the bebop players of the 1950s. His technique, too, was greeted with great admiration and even astonishment. Keeping his fingers relatively flat, rather than using the curved hand-shape favored by classical players, he gave the impression that his hands were barely moving. But despite his sheer speed, every note was clearly articulated and rhythmically precise.

In his own era he was not always so well-regarded. Some critics considered his playing too showy and overbearing. He was not a composer, choosing instead to radically reconfigure existing tunes from the standard repertoire, with some excursions into the light-classical area. Nor was he a great collaborator: he formed an influential trio in the 1940s, but for the most part he recorded alone, not least because of the difficulty other players had in keeping up with him.

A heavy drinker throughout his life, Tatum died in 1956 as a result of kidney failure. His reputation and influence, however, continued to grow. Today he is recognized as one of the most gifted musicians who ever lived. JM

Thelonious Monk

Thelonious Monk was eccentric in appearance, demeanor, and in his approach to the piano. Nonetheless, he has come to be recognized as one of the most important American musicians of the 20th century.

keyboard facts

◄ **Art Tatum**
Imaginative and technically gifted

Monk was born in North Carolina in 1917 and brought up in New York City. He took up piano at the age of nine, and seems to have had a year of lessons, but he was really self-taught: his mature style would owe nothing to classical technique. In the early 1940s he became the house pianist at Minton's Playhouse, the New York club where after-hours "cutting competitions" led directly to the creation of bebop, and began working with many of the new style's leading players, including Charlie Parker, Charlie Christian, Miles Davis, and Dizzy Gillespie. In 1944, he made his debut recordings, including the first account of one of his most celebrated compositions, "'Round Midnight." After working with Coleman Hawkins and Gillespie, he began to record as a leader from 1947, demonstrating his ability to create original material as the foundation for improvisation. Over the course of his career he wrote many tunes that have become jazz standards, including "Blue Monk," "Epistrophy," "Mysterioso," and "Straight, No Chaser."

▲ **Thelonious Monk**
Eccentric and inimitable

In 1951 he suffered a setback. Police searched a parked car in which Monk and his friend and fellow pianist Bud Powell were sitting and found drugs. Monk refused to testify against Powell and the police took away the essential "cabaret card" that he needed to be allowed to play in clubs in New York City. It took him six years to get it back, during which time his live appearances were severely restricted. He continued to record, with little commercial success, but a 1956 album, *Brilliant Corners*, with a highly complex title track, established his reputation. With his cabaret card restored, he suddenly found himself acclaimed as one of the most significant improvisers of the day.

In the 1960s his popularity was such that he signed to the giant Columbia record label and even became the cover star of *Time* magazine; the 1964 story made much of his eccentricities, which included wearing a variety of hats, standing up from the piano and turning slowly on the spot, and making cryptic remarks that defied analysis. It was his high point. As time went on his idiosyncrasies began to look more like serious mental illness, exacerbated by substance abuse. His last tour

the players

and recordings came in 1971, and for the last six years of his life he did not play at all, sitting mute in front of the television as a guest at the house of the heiress Baroness Pannonica de Koenigswarter, who had also nursed Charlie Parker through his last illness. He died in 1982 of a stroke.

Monk's style is immediately recognisable but not easily described: angular, percussive, sometimes discordant, and full of dramatic silences and idiosyncratic rhythmic displacements, it nonetheless owes as much to the venerable tradition of stride piano as it does to the bebop with which he was most associated. His influence remains huge, but through his compositions rather than his playing, which defies imitation. JM

▲ **Bud Powell**
The sound of bebop piano

Bud Powell

Earl Randolph "Bud" Powell was a virtuoso who brought to the piano the sound of bebop, pioneered by saxophonist Charlie Parker and trumpeter Dizzy Gillespie. Born in 1924 in New York City, he came from a musical household: his father played stride piano and his elder brother was a trumpeter. Bud began classical piano lessons at five, but by 10 had begun to imitate the stride style of Fats Waller and James P. Johnson. Later Thelonious Monk would become a great influence and mentor to the younger man.

In the early 1940s, Powell began playing in bands in New York City, where he took part in the jam sessions from which bebop emerged. Beginning as a disciple of Art Tatum, he soon developed a more spare style dominated by lighting-fast melodic lines in the right hand and minimal chording in the left. He had the ability to improvise single lines with the speed and fluency of the bebop wind players. Indeed, much of his best work was done in direct competition with the likes of Gillespie and Parker, with whom he enjoyed a combative relationship. In 1949 he formed his first trio with bass and drums, a format to which he returned repeatedly throughout his career. His compositions included "Hallucinations," "Un Poco Loco," "Dance Of The Infidels," and "Bouncing With Bud."

Sadly, Powell's life was scarred by recurrent mental illness, possibly precipitated by a beating he received from the police in 1945 while on tour in Philadelphia. He was repeatedly hospitalized and treated with electro-convulsive therapy and major tranquilizers. He was also an alcoholic, who would become belligerent, especially to other musicians, when drunk. It is often said that his best work was done before 1954, when his mental health and technical ability began to decline. In 1956 he moved to Paris, France, where he was adored by the French public, and somewhat recovered his reputation. This period inspired the 1986 movie *'Round Midnight*. In 1964 he returned to New York, and made a triumphant return to Birdland, the club that was one of his old haunts. But he soon succumbed to alcoholism once again and gave up music altogether. He died in 1966 from cirrhosis of the liver, after a long period of self-neglect. He was 41 years old. JM

Jimmy Smith

The Incredible Jimmy Smith, as he later became known, was the first star of the Hammond B-3 electric organ. He helped establish the organist's role in rhythm & blues and was a pioneer of what is now known as soul-jazz.

Born in Norristown, Pennsylvania, in 1925, Smith first started playing the Hammond in 1951 after graduating from the Ornstein School of Music. He spent the next few years performing in New York before starting his recording career with the Blue Note label in 1956. Among the dozens of albums he made for the label during the next seven years are *The Sermon!*, *The Champ*, and *Back at the Chicken Shack*, on which he worked with musicians including Kenny Burrell, Art Blakey, and Stanley Turrentine.

Smith wasn't the first jazz organist, but he was the first to demonstrate the full

keyboard facts

Jimmy Smith
Pioneer of soul-jazz

potential of the Hammond organ. Eschewing the big, heavy chords of previous organ-led groups, Smith developed a much punchier sound by playing basslines with his feet, swirling lower-register chords with his left hand, and fast, semi-improvised melodies with his right. His virtuoso playing helped to popularize the instrument and proved to be a major influence on the British and American blues stars of the 60s. By then Smith had moved to the Verve label, for whom he recorded a hit cover of Muddy Waters' "Got My Mojo Workin'" in 1966.

Smith's influence and popularity began to decline toward the end of the 60s, but there have been several resurgences of interest in his music in subsequent decades. He returned to Blue Note in the late 80s, and made two new albums for Verve in 1995. His last major album, released four years before his death in 2005, was *Dot Com Blues*, a Santana-like collaborative effort featuring contributions from B.B. King, Etta James, Taj Mahal, and other stars of blues, jazz, and soul.   TJS

Oscar Peterson

Oscar Peterson was a pianist of great gifts but also great dedication. Born in Montreal, Canada, in 1925, he began the serious study of classical piano at the age of eight and immediately applied himself to the scales and technical exercises he would practice all his life. At 14, he won a national talent contest organized by the Canadian Broadcasting Corporation, and shortly thereafter began his professional career as a player on radio and in hotels and music halls. Developing as a jazz pianist, his early influences included Nat "King" Cole and Art Tatum, although he once said that his first encounter with one of Tatum's records put him off playing for some weeks: "Tatum scared me to death," he recalled.

In 1949, the promoter Norman Granz invited him to appear at a Carnegie Hall concert in the "Jazz at the Philharmonic" series, and subsequently became his manager. In 1953 Peterson formed a trio with guitarist Herb Ellis and bassist Ray Brown. In 1958, Ellis was replaced by a drummer, Ed Thigpen, and that line-up continued until 1965. In the 1970s, Peterson began recording and performing as a solo artist and with symphony orchestras and important jazz artists of the day. Some felt that he did his best work as an accompanist, partnering such notable players as Lester Young, Stan Getz, Ben Webster, and Dizzy Gillespie.

He also composed and taught composition and improvisation, insisting that pianists study J.S. Bach alongside their jazz work. Best known as a master of the acoustic piano, he also recorded on electric piano, organ, and even clavichord.

In 1993, he suffered a severe stroke, causing paralysis on his left side, but was able to return to performance in a limited way later in the decade. He died in 2007 at his home in Mississauga, Ontario, Canada. A supreme technician, with an unerring sense of swing, Peterson is sometimes criticized for his lack of innovation over the course of his career, but he remains among the most admired players in all of jazz.   JM

Fats Domino

Antoine "Fats" Domino Jr. is often thought of in the context of the rock 'n' roll era, but in fact his career began some years earlier, and he continued to have hit records well into the 60s. In 1949, at the age of 21, he recorded his debut single, "The Fat Man." The song was only a minor hit (first locally, in his native New Orleans, and then nationally the following year), but was an important precursor to the piano-based rock 'n' roll that would become so prevalent in the 50s.

Domino's piano dominates the song, driving the rhythm and melody with rolling rhythm & blues chords. He continued to make records in much the same vein right through the 50s, hitting his commercial peak in 1957. He had five entries on the U.S. Top 10 that year including "Blue Monday," "I'm Walkin'," and "Blueberry Hill." His playing might not have been as inventive as that of some of his peers, but it would prove to be much copied, both during the 50s and beyond. The Beatles'

keyboard facts

Oscar Peterson
An unerring sense of swing

Fats Domino
Precursor of piano rock 'n' roll

"Lady Madonna" owed such a debt to Domino's style that he ended up recording his own version of it shortly after its release in 1968.

Domino's take on Paul McCartney's homage to his playing and singing scraped in at Number 100 on the *Billboard* singles chart. It proved to be his final US hit. By then his career as a record-maker had effectively ended, but in the years since his chart heyday he has received numerous Lifetime Achievement Awards and been inducted into various Halls of Fame. He returned to the public eye in 2005 when he went missing for several days after Hurricane Katrina hit New Orleans. Now in his 80s, he continues to perform at the yearly New Orleans Jazz & Heritage Festival and at other events in the vicinity of his hometown.   TJS

Bill Evans

William John Evans was born in Plainfield, New Jersey, in 1929, and began his training in classical piano at the age of six; he also played flute and violin. He left Southeastern Louisiana College in 1950 with a degree in piano performance and teaching.

▼ **Bill Evans**
Sensitive and self-effacing

By this time he had begun to play jazz and dance-band music, and after a spell in the U.S. Army he moved to New York and began pursuing a jazz career. In 1956 he made his first album, *New Jazz Conceptions*, which included "Waltz For Debby," one of his most famous compositions. But his real breakthrough came in 1958, when he was hired by Miles Davis. In his autobiography, Davis identified what he liked about Evans's playing: "Bill had this quiet fire that I loved on piano. The way he approached it, the sound he got was like crystal notes or sparkling water cascading down from some clear waterfall." He left the Davis sextet late in 1958, but returned early in 1959 to record *Kind of Blue*, one of the most influential of all jazz albums.

In 1959 he formed a trio with bassist Scott LaFaro and drummer Paul Motian which pioneered a kind of collective improvisation, and he would often return to the trio format throughout his life, as well as working on sessions with many of the great names of the day. In 1963 he broke new ground by double- and triple-tracking his piano for an album called *Conversations With Myself*. A sensitive and self-effacing man, Evans developed a style of exceptional intimacy, lyricism, and harmonic sophistication, with strong influences from 20th century classical music. His repertoire included many of his own compositions as well as standards, which he would comprehensively transform. In the course of his career he recorded some 600 hours of music, both in the studio and live.

Evans succumbed to heroin addiction in the late 1950s and fought it on and off for the rest of his life. In 1980, he began using cocaine, believing it to be less harmful. By this time his health was very poor and in September 1980 he died from a bleeding ulcer, cirrhosis of the liver, and bronchial pneumonia. He remains a colossal influence on jazz piano.   JM

Ray Charles

One of the most important figures in 20th-century popular music, Ray Charles played an integral role in the development of soul music.

Born in 1930 and blind since the age of six, Charles began his musical career in his late teens with the intention of trying to emulate the success—and vocal style—of Nat "King" Cole and Charles Brown. By the early 50s, however, he had come to realize that, in order to achieve lasting success, he needed to develop a style of his own.

In 1953 he formed a seven-piece band—piano, bass, and drums, plus two saxophones and two trumpets—and started to experiment with a mixture of rhythm & blues, and gospel.

Charles had his first major hit a year later with "I Got a Woman," which topped the *Billboard* R&B chart, and which he followed over the next few years with such landmark recordings as "Mess Around" and "Night Time is the Right Time." It wasn't until 1959, however, that he truly made his mark on the mainstream market. Running to six-and-a-half minutes—more than twice the length of most pop records of the time—the million-selling "What'd I Say" broke all sorts of boundaries, not least in the way that its call-and-response vocals were, as Charles himself would later put it, "all about the sounds of making love."

Perhaps the most important element of the song, however, is Charles's electric-piano playing. His series of deft runs and riffs in E major might not sound particularly remarkable to modern ears, but their familiarity serves only to show how great an impact Charles had on subsequent musicians.

Charles continued to innovate throughout the 60s, recording definitive versions of songs such as "Georgia on My Mind" and "Hit the Road Jack" and helping to popularize country music with the 1965 album *Modern Sounds in Country and Western Music*. Although the quality of his work had started to slip by the start of the 70s, he continued to write, record, and perform right up until his death in 2004.   TJS

▲ **Ray Charles**
Breaking all sorts of boundaries

Joe Zawinul

One of the preeminent composers and keyboardists of jazz fusion, Zawinul played with and helped revolutionize the sound of groups led by Cannonball Adderley and Miles Davis before cofounding Weather Report and the Zawinul Syndicate.

Born in 1932 in Vienna, Austria, Zawinul moved to the United States in 1959 to study at Berklee College of Music. Within a couple of years, having already played with Dinah Washington, he had joined the Cannonball Adderley Quintet, with whom he worked throughout the 60s. He wrote several of Adderley's biggest hits of the decade, including "Mercy, Mercy, Mercy," a Number 11 hit on the *Billboard* pop chart in 1967. By then he had become one of the first jazz keyboardists to switch from acoustic piano to the Fender Rhodes, which brought a heavier timbre to his playing. For a time Zawinul worked closely with Harold Rhodes, the inventor of the instrument, to help refine the sound and feel of it.

In 1968 Zawinul started playing with Miles Davis, whom he had known for some years and who had already recorded one of his most famous compositions, "Directions," in 1960. Zawinul became the third keyboardist in Davis's electric group of the late 60s. With Chick Corea and Herbie Hancock already playing electric pianos, Zawinul switched to organ for such landmark recordings as *In a Silent Way* (for which he wrote the title track) and *Bitches Brew*. Tending mostly to follow the shapes and patterns of the bassline, his contributions to Davis's ensemble were simple but decidedly effective.

In the 70s, Zawinul made the jump from sideman to bandleader with Weather Report, the group he formed with another of Davis's 60s bandmates, saxophonist Wayne Shorter. Experimenting with early synthesizers such as the ARP 2600 on albums including *Sweetnighter* (1973) and *Heavy Weather* (1978), Weather Report

keyboard facts

◀ **Joe Zawinul**
Preminent in jazz-fusion

helped bridge the gap between progressive rock and jazz. After the group split in the mid 80s, Zawinul formed the more world-music-orientated Zawinul Syndicate and wrote a symphony, *Stories of the Danube*. He died in 2007 at the age 75, having over the years won *Down Beat* magazine's yearly Best Keyboardist award an incredible 30 times. TJS

Little Richard

Perhaps the most important and influential star of the rock 'n' roll era, Little Richard has been named as a major source of inspiration by everyone from Elvis Presley and Otis Redding to Paul McCartney and David Bowie. This has a lot to do with his extravagant showmanship and manic singing style, but can also be attributed to his fierce, rhythmic piano-playing.

Born in 1932, as Richard Penniman, Richard has been performing since the 40s, but he is most famous for the records he made during a brief period in the mid to late 50s—a run of hits that included "Tutti Fruti," "Good Golly Miss Molly," and "Long Tall Sally." After appearing at medicine shows as a "healer" in his teenage years, Richard signed his first recording contract in 1951 and started cutting records that drew on his love of gospel and rhythm & blues, and in particular the work of two flamboyant, pioneering stars of the 40s and 50s: the singer Billy Wright, and the pianist Esquerita. He didn't achieve widespread success, however, until he was discovered by Art Rupe of Specialty Records in 1955.

the players

▲ **Little Richard**
Inspirational rock 'n' roll

In the space of the next couple of years Richard cut some of the defining works of the rock 'n' roll era and appeared in several landmark movies of the period, including *The Girl Can't Help It* and *Don't Knock the Rock*. By the end of 1957, however, he had decided to bring his career to a sudden close, opting instead to devote his time and energy to evangelism. For the next few decades he flitted between rock 'n' roll—which included playing with The Beatles and Jimi Hendrix—and the church. It wasn't until 1986, the year that he was inducted into the Rock 'n' Roll Hall Of Fame, that he found himself able to reconcile his twin callings by cutting an album of inspirational rock 'n' roll. He has continued to perform and preach, and remains one of the 20th century's most respected stars.   TJS

Jerry Lee Lewis

Few stars of the rock 'n' roll era were given so apt a nickname as "The Killer." But as well as being one of the period's most combustible, controversial stars, Lewis was also one of its finest and most influential pianists.

Born in 1935, Lewis demonstrated an affinity for the piano at a young age, and by his teenage years seemed to have hit upon his own, high-energy take on boogie-woogie playing. In the early 50s he was sent by his mother to Bible college in Waxahachie, Texas, but was reportedly expelled for playing "the devil's music."

In 1956, after being discovered by producer/engineer Jack Clement, he became an integral part of the Sun Records stable, playing on hits by artists including Billy Lee Riley and Carl Perkins. By then he had already developed a fearsome reputation for his own performances as Jerry Lee Lewis and His Pumping Piano, which seemed to have as much to do with his frantic onstage behavior—notably his tendency to kick away his piano stool and play standing up—as it did with his playing style, which generally entails hammering out a solid rhythmic foundation with his left hand and adding bold, ostentatious touches with his right.

Lewis reached his peak in 1957 with the release of "Whole Lotta Shakin' Goin' On" and "Great Balls of Fire." Within a year, however, his career hit a major point of crisis after it was revealed in the British press that he was married to a 13-year-old first cousin (once removed). Support for the man and his music quickly disappeared, and he went from playing huge rock 'n' roll concerts to small clubs.

Despite this and other controversies, Lewis is widely thought of as one of the greatest stars of the rock 'n' roll era. In 1986 he was among the first inductees to the Rock and Roll Hall of Fame and Museum, and three years later became the subject of a major biopic, *Great Balls Of Fire*, starring Dennis Quaid and Winona Ryder. He has continued to make records and perform live. His 2008 duet with Little Richard—a medley of "Great Balls of Fire" and "Good Golly Miss Molly"—was one of the highlights of the 50th Grammy Awards show.   TJS

Garth Hudson

As the principal keyboardist in The Band, and perhaps its most integral member, Hudson helped change the course of North American rock 'n' roll in the late 60s and early 70s. In 1961, after playing for a few years in The Capers, he was the last of five musicians to join Ronnie Hawkins's backing band, The Hawks. (At 24, he was also the oldest of the players by some distance.)

The musicians split with Hawkins a couple of years later and began working on material of their own. Before becoming The Band and recording *Music from Big Pink*, however, the group made a series of legendary recordings with Bob Dylan (taped by Hudson) that resulted in what are now known as *The Basement Tapes*.

Although all five members contributed to the sound of The Band, Hudson was often at the forefront. While most rock 'n' roll keyboardists of the time played Hammond organs, Hudson preferred the sound and feel of the lesser-known Lowrey brand. The expansive material on *Music from Big Pink* gave him the

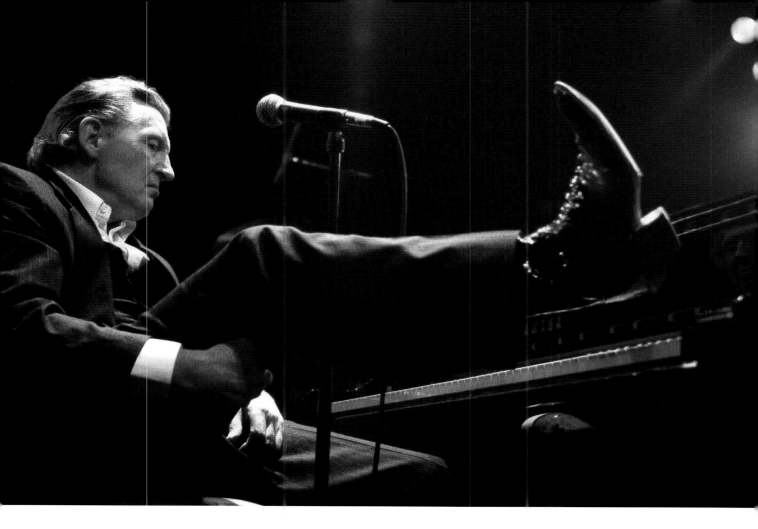

opportunity to show off the full range of his playing ability, from spacious chords on "Tears of Rage" to driving lead work on "Chest Fever."

Another crucial aspect of his playing with The Band was the way that he interacted with pianist Richard Manuel—another fine player whose deft, melodic touch lay at the heart of many of the group's best songs. Prior to The Band's emergence, few rock 'n' roll acts had contained more than one keyboard player.

Primarily thought of as an organist, Hudson played a number of other instruments with The Band including saxophone and accordion. He pioneered the concept of playing a Clavinet through a wah-wah pedal on the 1969 track "Up on Cripple Creek" and began experimenting with synthesizers toward the end of the original line-up's time together in the mid 70s. Since then he has established himself as a highly sought-after session musician, and has worked with everyone from Eric Clapton and Leonard Cohen to Mercury Rev and Wilco. TJS

Ray Manzarek

With The Doors, Ray Manzarek (born 1939) established himself as one of the most distinctive keyboard players of the rock era. What set him apart from his peers was his choice of instrument as much as his playing style.

"I didn't want to use a Hammond organ," Manzarek told *Keyboard* magazine in 1991, "because I didn't want to sound like Jimmy Smith." He opted instead for the tinny, wheezy sound of the Vox Continental, and drew on a wide range of influences that included Claude Debussy, Bill Evans, and Johnnie Johnson, who played the piano on—and inspired the title of—Chuck Berry's seminal hit "Johnny B. Goode."

Another important influence on his playing style was the makeup of The Doors. The group lacked a permanent bassist, so Manzarek ended up filling out the low end with lines played on a Fender Rhodes keyboard bass, leaving only his right hand to play the Vox. As such he rarely played chords but focused on nagging, insistent lead lines instead.

Although he is known primarily for the kind of swirling motifs that dominate the

▲ **Jerry Lee Lewis**
High-energy boogie-woogie

▼ **Garth Hudson**
Preferred Lowrey over Hammond

the players

seven-minute "Light My Fire" (1967), Manzarek was capable of adopting a more subtle approach when required. This side of his playing is best exemplified by the jazzy, psychedelic "Riders on the Storm" (1971)—the last song The Doors recorded together. By then he had also begun to use a Hammond on occasion, having been given a C-3 model for his birthday by bandmates Jim Morrison and Robby Krieger. He also used a harpsichord on several Doors recordings, including "Love Me Two Times" and "Can You Give Me Sanctuary."

In the years since the dissolution of The Doors, Manzarek has followed a singular career path that has seen him produce Generation X, the punk group led by Billy Idol, record his own jazz-rock take on *Carmina Burana*, and collaborate with the composer Philip Glass. But nothing he has played since has come close to the impact of the cheap, cheesy organ sound first heard on *The Doors*.   TJS

Herbie Hancock

In a career spanning five decades, Herbie Hancock has revolutionized the role of the jazz keyboardist and made pioneering use of synthesizers.

Born in 1940, Hancock played on a number of Blue Note sessions during the early 60s before being invited to join what became known as Miles Davis's "second great quintet" in 1963. He quickly established a playing style that set him apart from any other jazz pianist, adding unusual chords and Debussy-like melodies to albums such as *E.S.P.* (1965) and *Miles Smiles* (1966). By the summer of 1968 he had begun to experiment with using a Fender Rhodes electric piano, as heard on *Miles in the Sky*, *Filles de Kilimanjaro*, and the landmark *In a Silent Way*, on which his ethereal playing merges beautifully with that of two other legendary keyboardists, Chick Corea and Joe Zawinul.

▼ **Ray Manzarek**
With The Doors

Although he continued to play on studio sessions with Davis until 1972, Hancock had left Miles's group by the time *In a Silent Way* was released in October 1969. In 1971, having already formed a sextet of his own, he met Dr. Patrick Gleeson, who introduced him to the world of synthesizers and sequencing. The albums *Crossings* (1972) and *Sextant* (1973) were among the first jazz albums to explore the possibilities of instruments such as the ARP Odyssey and the Moog III. A year later Hancock formed the jazz-funk group Head Hunters and had one of his biggest hits with a heavily synthesized album of the same name.

Hancock spent much of the rest of the 70s working on solo projects, but also lent his talents to recordings by Stevie Wonder, Jaco Pastorius, and Quincy Jones. "Rockit," his 1983 collaboration with bassist and producer Bill Laswell, programmer Michael Beinhorn, and turntablist Grand Mixer DXT, was one the first hit records to feature DJ-scratching. Hancock has continued to tour and record into the 21st century, and has worked with a wide array of contemporary stars including Christina Aguilera, Norah Jones, and Corinne Bailey Rae.   TJS

▲ **Herbie Hancock**
Debussy-like melodies

Giorgio Moroder

A sequencer is a computer that "plays" keyboards and other electronic instruments by "instructing" them what musical notes to sound, and when to sound them. In the 1970s sequencers were standalone modules, though now they are part of most music-making software packages, and are included in workstation keyboards. The German-based producer, musician and songwriter Giorgio Moroder, born in 1940 in Italy, began his musical career as a bassist and guitarist but became one of the first people to harness the potential of sequencers as music-making tools. In doing so he created a style of keyboard "performance" that continues to dominate much commercial dance music, and virtually every techno record ever made. He qualifies for these pages more as a keyboard *user* than a keyboard *player*.

Moroder had dabbled with synthesizers almost as soon as they became commercially available, and was the brains behind an early synth novelty hit, "Son Of My Father," by Chicory Tip (1972). But his defining moment came with Donna Summer's electro-disco epic, "I Feel Love" (1977). The song's backing track was entirely electronic, built on a mesmerizing bass synth pulse that was sequenced, not played. Indeed, given the speed of the part and the length of the song (six minutes), playing it conventionally was impossible, although Summer appeared on TV many times with her live band gamely miming to the song with a conventional drums, keyboards, and guitar line-up.

In the course of his career, Moroder has worked with a wide range of artists, including Barbra Streisand, Elton John, Cher, Janet Jackson, David Bowie, Blondie, Sparks, Roger Daltry, and Phil Oakey of the Human League. He has also written and produced numerous movie scores, winning three Academy Awards.   MB

▲ **Giorgio Moroder**
Harnessing the sequencer

Chick Corea

The son of a jazz trumpeter, Chick Corea was born in 1941 in Chelsea, Massachusetts. He studied classical composition in his teenage years before becoming a prominent fusion keyboardist. After working during the early to mid 60s with acts including Herbie Mann and Stan Getz, Corea was invited to take the place of Herbie Hancock in Miles Davis's band in 1968. He made his first recorded appearance with Davis on that year's *Filles de Kilimanjaro*. While he plays acoustic piano on the opening "Frelon Brun," by the time of the closing "Mademoiselle Mabry" he had made the important symbolic switch to the RMI Electra-piano (with which he often used a ring modulation effect).

On the follow-up album, *In a Silent Way* (1969), he is one of three legendary keyboard players. With Hancock adding atmospheric melodic touches on Fender Rhodes and Joe Zawinul filling out the low-end on organ, Corea takes a more rhythmic approach. His playing is more prominent on *Bitches Brew*, on which he is the only keyboardist to appear on all six tracks and a soloist on "Miles Runs the Voodoo Down."

After leaving Davis's group in 1970, Corea formed the free-jazz quintet Circle. He subsequently pursued a different type of jazz-fusion in the Latin-tinged group Return to Forever. In recent years he has moved away from jazz toward classical composition. He wrote his first piano concerto in 1999 and has adapted some of his past jazz works (notably "Spain") for orchestra. He is also a prominent Scientologist, and regularly cites L. Ron Hubbard as a continuing influence on his writing and playing.   TJS

▼ **Chick Corea**
A different type of jazz-fusion

▲ **Jon Lord**
Bringing Hammond to hard rock

Jon Lord

Jon Lord is notable for bringing the jazzy sound of the Hammond organ into the heart of rock music through his work with Deep Purple and Whitesnake. Born in 1941 in Leicester, England, he began learning classical piano at the age of five, but later came to love the jazz organ sounds of Jimmy Smith, Brother Jack McDuff, and others. His original ambition was to be an actor, but in the long gaps between parts he made ends meet by playing piano and organ in clubs and sessions.

Various false starts in music led in 1968 to the formation of Deep Purple, an early hard-rock band to which Lord was determined to bring the Hammond organ. To make a sound that could compete with Richie Blackmore's electric guitar, he took to playing the Hammond through Marshall amplifiers with shattering results. At the same time, he pursued an interest in fusing rock with classical music, leading to his *Concerto for Group and Orchestra*, performed live in 1969 and later released as an album.

The classical experiment was not universally popular within the group, and subsequent albums saw Deep Purple developing into the template for the heavy rock that would follow. Lord's baroque-influenced playing is particularly notable on tracks such as "Speed King" and "Child in Time," from *Deep Purple in Rock*, and "Highway Star" and "Space Truckin'" from *Machine Head*. At the same time, he continued to pursue his interest in orchestral composition outside the confines of the band, which split in 1976.

Lord subsequently joined Whitesnake, where he employed a Yamaha electric grand piano as well as a rack of Moog synthesizers, but he considered himself no more than a hired hand. In 1984, Deep Purple reformed and Lord reinstalled himself behind the Hammond before retiring in September 2002. He has since enjoyed a low-key but rewarding solo career that has ranged from rhythm & blues to orchestral works. His latest work in that vein, the *Durham Concerto*, was premiered in 2007 in the city of Durham, England.   JM

Alan Price

A founding member of The Animals, Alan Price played on one of the most memorable hits of the 60s—and perhaps the first ever folk-rock hit—"House of the Rising Sun."

Born in 1942, he taught himself to play the organ at a young age and in his teens played the church organ in his town of Jarrow, in the north of England. In the early 60s he formed The Alan Price Rhythm & Blues Combo, which subsequently became The Animals with the addition of vocalist Eric Burdon. In June 1964 the group released their swirling, hypnotic take on the American standard "House of the Rising Sun" (previously recorded by Bob Dylan among others).

Price arranged the song, and his rich, expressive organ-playing is at its heart. "I use a lot more chords than most organists," he told *Melody Maker* a year later, "and I'm careful to phrase them with the guitar. I tend to think of the organ as part of the rhythm section, rather than a frontline voice." On this and other early Animals

keyboard facts

Alan Price
On Vox Continental with The Animals

Georgie Fame
Highly versatile, with a relaxed style

▲ **Rick Wright**
A subtle, complementary style

hits he plays a Vox Continental, the most famous of the new breed of lightweight transistor organs to emerge in the early 60s.

Price left The Animals in 1965 after falling out with Burdon. He formed The Alan Price Set shortly thereafter and had hits over the next few years with covers of "I Put a Spell On You" and "Simon Smith and his Amazing Dancing Bear." In 1971 he recorded an album in collaboration with another noted British organist, Georgie Fame, which yielded the Top 20 hit "Rosetta." He has also written movie soundtracks and worked as an actor, most notably in *Alfie Darling*, the 1975 sequel to *Alfie*.   TJS

Georgie Fame

Born Clive Powell in Leigh, Lancashire, England, in 1943, Fame acquired his new name when he signed a management contract with impresario Larry Parnes. Parnes always renamed his artists: other examples included Billy Fury and Marty Wilde.

Fame, who began learning piano at seven, was 16 at the time and already playing with The Blue Flames, backing band for Fury. In 1961, band and singer parted company. The Blue Flames (later Georgie Fame and The Blue Flames) carried on, taking up a three-year residency at The Flamingo, a London club central to the developing British rhythm & blues scene, and achieving UK Number One hits with "Yeh Yeh" and "Getaway." In 1968, "The Ballad of Bonnie and Clyde," attributed to Georgie Fame alone, was a hit in both Britain and the U.S.

Starting as an out-and-out rock 'n' roll pianist, influenced by Jerry Lee Lewis, Fame soon adopted a jazzier style and began using a Hammond organ. Between 1970 and 1973, he teamed up with fellow keyboard player Alan Price. The pair achieved a hit with "Rosetta" and were so popular that they had their own BBC television series. In 1974, Fame reformed The Blue Flames: the band has continued to work with him, in various line-ups, to this day.

In the 1980s he worked on various jazz-based projects as player, producer, and

keyboard facts

singer, and then in 1989 he joined Van Morrison's band as organist, having previously worked on Morrison's album *Avalon Sunset*. He remained with Morrison throughout most of the 1990s, as well as continuing to record his own albums. In 1997, Bill Wyman formed his band The Rhythm Kings and Fame joined as a founder member, again on organ and vocals. The band has released five albums and toured intermittently ever since.

A highly versatile musician, with a relaxed style reflecting his interest in both jazz and rhythm & blues, Fame continues to perform solo, and also with jazz groups, rock bands, big bands, and orchestras. Over the years he has played and recorded with artists as varied as Count Basie, Gene Vincent, Muddy Waters, Eric Clapton, Prince Buster, Joan Armatrading, and The Verve.   JM

Rick Wright

As the principal keyboardist in Pink Floyd, Rick Wright helped fashion some of the best-loved rock music of all time. Born in 1943, he cofounded the group in 1965 with Roger Waters and Nick Mason, with whom he had studied at the Regent Street Polytechnic College of Architecture in the early 60s. He wrote—and sang—several of the group's earliest songs, but since then his primary focus has been to add color and texture to the group's sound.

Unlike many of his peers in the progressive-rock world, Wright tended to favor a subtle, complementary style, with solos being the exception rather than the rule. To begin with he mostly played a Farfisa organ (often through an echo unit), but as the group's sound as a whole became ever more expansive he responded in kind by bringing in a host of new keyboard instruments. Among his most distinctive contributions to the group's catalog are the overlapping Moogs on "Any Colour You Like," the jazzy Wurlitzer chords on "Money," and the ghostly piano lines fed through a Leslie speaker on "Echoes."

By the late 70s Wright's arsenal of keyboards also included Fender Rhodes and Hohner electric pianos, Hammond organ, harmonium, and various EMS, ARP, and Prophet 5 synthesizers. (He replaced many of these during the 80s and 90s with Kurzweil digital keyboards capable of reproducing the original analog sounds.) But for all his experimentation, some of Wright's finest moments are played simply on acoustic piano without any special effects, notably *Dark Side of the Moon*'s stately centerpiece, "The Great Gig in the Sky."   TJS

Larry Tamblyn

The Standells were one of the most successful of the many garage-punk bands to emerge from the U.S. in the mid 60s, their career stretching to several albums and national hit singles. Larry Tamblyn, born in 1943 in Los Angeles, was a founding and ever-present member in a shifting line-up, his organ riffs a distinctive feature of the band's sound.

Formed in 1962 as a dance hall covers act, The Standells waited four years before their first hit, "Dirty Water," climbed to Number 11 on the *Billboard* charts. The song is a neat summation of not just the Standells' sound, but the whole garage rock style, a distinct Rolling Stones influence pervading its mildly anti-establishment lyrics and repetitive, simplistic riff. That riff was doubled up on guitar and Tamblyn's Vox organ, and much of the organist's subsequent work in the band followed that pattern: basic, and primarily rhythmic rather than melodic. It was a style that Tamblyn shared with many others, and it crops up on most of the genre's other greatest hits. Take ? and The Mysterians classic "96 Tears," a number one hit in 1966. The song is dominated by a stabbing major/minor organ riff played by Frank Rodriguez, just 14 years old at the time.

The garage organ sound—generally courtesy of Farfisa or Vox—the playing style, and, incidentally, the stance (always standing, never sitting, at the keyboard),

▲ **Larry Tamblyn**
With The Standells

the players

has since become embedded in rock's language. Many American new-wave bands revived it in the late 70s, with Blondie's Jimmy Destri being a prime exponent. A decade or so later, Manchester baggy band Inspiral Carpets had many organ-driven hits. Now, most sound modules and software synths will have presets labeled "garage organ" or something similar.   MB

Keith Emerson

Perhaps the finest Hammond player of the progressive-rock era, Keith Emerson is best known for his work with the "supergroup" he formed with Greg Lake and Carl Palmer in 1970.

Born in 1944, Emerson first rose to prominence in his early 20s as the leader of The Nice before forming Emerson, Lake & Palmer (ELP) with bassist Lake (formerly of King Crimson) and drummer Palmer (from Atomic Rooster). Although he was the primary songwriter in both groups, he derived much of his material from classical compositions. His work with The Nice included interpretations of pieces by Bach, Sibelius, and Leonard Bernstein, while his best known recording with ELP is the group's album-length live rendition of Mussorgsky's *Pictures at an Exhibition* (1971).

By then Emerson had become notorious for his idiosyncratic and often violent playing style. As well as incorporating layers of feedback and distortion into his sound, he would stab knives into the keys of his Hammond organ to hold down notes during the wild, Hendrix-inspired solos of tracks such as "Hoedown" (adapted from a piece by Aaron Copland).

Emerson is known primarily for his Hammond playing, but was also the first musician to incorporate a Moog into his live setup. By the mid 70s his onstage arsenal included two Hammonds (a C-3 and an L-100), a Steinway concert grand, an upright piano, a Clavinet, and several Moogs (often with a ribbon controller attached to one of them).

Unlike many of his peers, Emerson has maintained a keen interest in new developments in keyboard technologies. In 1976 he reportedly paid $50,000 for a brand new Yamaha GX-1 synthesizer, while he has also worked extensively with Korg instruments.   TJS

▼ **Keith Emerson**
A consummate showman

keyboard facts

Keith Jarrett

One of the most prolific jazz pianists of the past half-century, Jarrett has worked with Art Blakey and Miles Davis, led countless groups of his own, and made significant excursions into classical, blues, folk, and world music.

Born in Allentown, Pennsylvania, in 1945, Jarrett got his break in mid-60s New York playing with Art Blakey's Jazz Messengers. He then became a member of the Charles Lloyd Quartet before being invited to play with Miles Davis in 1970. Although he favors acoustic instruments, and later claimed to be on an "anti-electric-music crusade," Jarrett played two Fender keyboards in Davis's group, alternating, with Chick Corea, between a Contempo organ and a Rhodes electric piano. His impassioned playing can be heard on *At Fillmore*, *Live/Evil*, *Get Up With It*, and various later compilations and *Complete Sessions* collections.

◄ **Keith Jarrett**
Playing it straight

During the mid 70s Jarrett became hugely successful as a solo pianist. *The Köln Concert*, a live recording of four lengthy, completely improvised pieces, sold more than three million copies upon its release in 1975, making it one of the most successful jazz records of all time. It serves as a prime example of his incredible knack for taking a simple one-chord vamp and drawing all manner of melodic and counterpointal material from it. (The first half of "Part II A," for example, is played over the same repeating figure in A major.)

By then Jarrett had become famous as much for the way that he played as the music he made. Shifting and shaking, grunting and groaning, and frequently sliding off the piano stool, he was later described by the *New York Times* as "look[ing] as though he were giving birth to a square baby." But he is capable of playing it straight, too, as evidenced by his more recent forays into classical music, which have taken in well-received recordings and performances of works by Bach, Shostakovich, Mozart, and the Estonian minimalist Arvo Pärt.   TJS

Booker T. Jones

The leader of one of the world's first racially integrated soul bands, Memphis-born Jones is responsible for some of the most distinctive Hammond playing in the history of popular music.

Although he is best known as an organist, Jones made his recorded debut in 1961 when he played baritone sax on "Cause I Love You" by Rufus and Carla

the players

Thomas. He was only 16 at the time, but by then had already learned to play the saxophone, oboe, trumpet, and piano. By the time he left high school he had met guitarist Steve Cropper, formed the instrumental soul group Booker T. & The MGs, and written the landmark hit "Green Onions."

"Green Onions" serves as a prime example of the kind of laid-back, unfussy playing that Jones is best known for. But despite the huge success of the single (a number three hit on *Billboard*) and its parent album, *Green Onions*, Jones elected to continue his musical education through to the mid 60s, studying composition at Indiana University during the week and returning home to play with the MGs at weekends.

While it looked for a while like Booker T. & The MGs might never have another hit of their own, the group soon became one of the 60s finest house bands, playing on numerous chart-smashes for other Stax acts including Otis Redding, Sam & Dave, and Albert King, whose "Born Under a Bad Sign" Jones co-wrote. Then in 1967 the group returned to the charts with "Hip-Hug-Her," the first song to feature Jones playing a Hammond B-3. It was the first of a run of hits that also included "Time is Tight," "Soul Limbo," and the effortlessly funky "Melting Pot."

Although Jones and his MGs have played together less regularly since the 70s, they have been reunited on various occasions since—albeit without drummer Al Jackson Jr., who died in 1975—and have backed a wide array of stars over the years including Bob Dylan, Neil Young, and Stevie Wonder. TJS

▼ **Booker T. Jones**
Laid-back and unfussy

keyboard facts

◄ **Billy Preston**
Equal billing with The Beatles

Billy Preston

Over the years, the name "the fifth Beatle" has been given to everyone from Muhammed Ali to Neil Aspinall. But few deserve the title more than Billy Preston, the rhythm & blues keyboardist who played on the albums *Let It Be* and *Abbey Road* and was given equal billing on the transatlantic number one hit "Get Back."

Born in 1946, Preston first met The Beatles in 1962 while playing in Little Richard's band. By the time he was invited to contribute to the *Get Back* sessions by George Harrison seven years later he had also worked extensively with Ray Charles and recorded several solo albums, notably *The Wildest Organ in Town* (1966), which features arrangements by a pre-fame Sly Stone. He was also part of the house band on the mid-60s ABC-TV show *Shindig!* alongside Glen Campbell and noted session-pianist Leon Russell.

Preston played Hammond and Fender Rhodes on a number of the songs that ended up on The Beatles' swansong, *Let It Be*, and on *Abbey Road*'s "Something" and "I Want You (She's So Heavy)." He also took part of the group's last live performance, on the roof of the Apple building at 3 Savile Row, London.

His career as a solo artist peaked in the years directly following his association with The Beatles. He topped the *Billboard* singles chart with "Will it go Round in Circles" and "Nothing From Nothing" and won a Grammy Award for the Clavinet-led "Outa-Space." He also cowrote "You are so Beautiful," later a hit for Joe Cocker. Although his popularity began to decline after the mid 70s, Preston continued to perform on stage and on record until 2005. (He died in 2006.) The long list of big-name stars he collaborated with along the way includes Bob Dylan, Elton John, The Jackson 5, The Red Hot Chili Peppers, and three of four solo Beatles: Harrison, Lennon, and Starr.

TJS

the players

Steve Winwood

As both bandleader and session-player, Steve Winwood was one of the most prominent and talented Hammond players of the 60s and 70s. Born in 1948, he became a key player on the Birmingham, England, rhythm & blues scene while still at school, and by the time he reached his teenage years had backed all manner of visiting U.S. stars such as Muddy Waters, Chuck Berry, and Bo Diddley.

At 15 Winwood joined The Spencer Davis Group on keyboards and vocals. He promptly cowrote the hits "Gimme Some Lovin'" (1966) and "I'm a Man" (1967) both of which are driven by his swirling, expressive keyboard-playing and rich vocal delivery. By April 1967, however, he had left Davis's side to form Traffic with drummer Jim Capaldi, guitarist Dave Mason, and flautist and saxophonist Chris Wood. The group's career started strongly with a run of three UK hit singles— "Paper Sun," "Hole in My Shoe," and "Here We Go Round the Mulberry Bush"— that showed off a more expansive, psychedelic sound. By the end of the 60s, however, Winwood seemed to have become more interested in playing with other acts, lending his expressive organ-playing to Joe Cocker's hit cover of The Beatles' "With a Little Help from My Friends," and album sessions for Jimi Hendrix and Howlin' Wolf. He also cofounded Blind Faith, the shortlived blues-rock group led by Eric Clapton.

Then, in 1970, Winwood brought back Capaldi and Wood to help complete an album he had originally intended to be his solo debut, but which ended up being Traffic's defining work. *John Barleycorn Must Die* showcased a more restrained, jazz-rock sound that belied the fact that its principal creator was still only 22 years old. Having reached what most critics feel to be his creative peak so young, Winwood had to wait almost two decades for his greatest commercial success. His late-80s reinvention as a blue-eyed soul singer yielded a run of international hit albums and two U.S. chart-topping singles, "Higher Love" and "Roll With It." TJS

Rick Wakeman

One of the most inventive and extravagant keyboardists of the progressive-rock era, Rick Wakeman (born 1949) had originally planned to train as a concert pianist until he was kicked out of London's Royal College of Music for neglecting his studies. His introduction to the world of electronic keyboards was rather serendipitous. In the late 60s the young British actor Jack Wild (best known for his role in *Oliver!*) decided to sell Wakeman his newly purchased Minimoog, unhappy at the fact that it only played one note at a time.

By then Wakeman had begun to make his name as a session musician, appearing on a number of hits of the late 60s and early 70s including "Space Oddity" and "Changes" by David Bowie and "Morning Has Broken" by Cat Stevens. He also played on two albums by The Strawbs. In 1971 he was invited to join Yes as a replacement for Tony Kaye, who had been resistant to his bandmates' desire for him to play something else aside from the Hammond organ. Wakeman duly obliged, filling out the group's breakthrough album, *Fragile* (1972), with everything from Moog to Mellotron.

Wakeman played a similarly important role in the making of the group's next two albums, *Close to the Edge* and the two-disc set *Tales from Topographic Oceans*, but left shortly thereafter to pursue a solo career. He has made dozens of albums in the years since, the most memorable among them being the great rock folly of *Myths and Legends of King Arthur and the Knights of the Round Table*. The album itself was reasonably successful and well received by critics, but was overshadowed by the excesses of the supporting tour, a grand theatrical production on ice. Despite being a sellout, the stage show proved so expensive that it led to Wakeman having to file for bankruptcy.

After recovering from that setback, and from a series of heart attacks brought

Steve Winwood
Expressive keyboards and soulful vocals

Rick Wakeman
Inventive and extravagant

Roland D-50

▲ **Dave Greenfield**
With The Stranglers

on by alcohol abuse, he has reestablished himself as a solo artist and soundtrack composer. He has also returned to live and studio work with Yes from time to time, and is the Honorary President of the UK's Classic Rock Society. TJS

Dave Greenfield

Although not a household name by any stretch of the imagination, Dave Greenfield is notable as being one of the few prominent keyboardists of the punk-rock era. In 1975, at the age of 26, he joined the classic line-up of The Stranglers alongside bassist/vocalist Jean-Jacques Burnel, guitarist/vocalist Hugh Cornwell, and drummer Brian "Jet Black" Duffy, and quickly set about making his mark with a fast, arpeggiated style that has regularly been compared to the playing of The Doors' Ray Manzarek.

In the late 70s, while most groups of the time limited themselves to a few scratchy guitar chords, bass, and drums, Greenfield embellished The Stranglers' songs with up-tempo flourishes of Hohner Cembalet electric piano ("Peaches"), Hammond L-100 organ (a jaunty rendition of "Walk On By"), and MiniMoog ("No More Heroes"). By the start of the 80s, with his bandmates delving into the murky world of the concept album on *The Gospel According to the Meninblack*, Greenfield had begun to dabble in even more left-field techniques—including using a Korg VC-10 Vocoder—that set the group even further apart from their punk rock peers.

In 1982 Hugh Cornwell took a piece of music Greenfield had written during the *Meninblack* sessions and turned it into The Stranglers' biggest ever hit, "Golden Brown." (As if any further evidence is needed that this was not your average bunch of punk rockers, the song is a harpsichord-led waltz that alternates between 3/4 and 4/4 in its chorus.) TJS

keyboard facts

Roy Bittan

The balding, bespectacled "Professor," as Roy Bittan is known, was born in New York City in 1949. He joined Bruce Springsteen's E Street Band in 1974. Notwithstanding the periods when the band has been inactive, he has been a member ever since. Although he has used organs and synthesizers, and is a skilled accordionist, his most recognizable contribution is as a pianist. Indeed, for most of its existence The E Street Band has featured two keyboard players, Bittan on piano, and the late Danny Federici on organ.

Bittan's playing on Springsteen's ballads is generally conventional, but he can be credited with inventing a new style of rock piano for the fast songs. Before Bittan, most fast rock piano was rhythmic and percussive. Playing on uptempo late 60s Rolling Stones and Beatles songs, for example, clearly harked back to the 1950s pounding chords of Jerry Lee Lewis and Little Richard. In contrast, Bittan introduced a more melodic style, euphoric and rousing, using arpeggios and occasional grandiose flourishes like a rock 'n' roll Liberace. The early Springsteen classic, "Thunder Road" (1976) is a prime example of Bittan in full flow.

The style would become a trademark of American rock in the 80s and 90s. It is much copied by other players, and apart from Springsteen, Bittan himself has played on dozens of hit albums by the likes of David Bowie, Tracy Chapman, Chicago, Dire Straits, Peter Gabriel, Meat Loaf, Stevie Nicks, and Bon Jovi.   MB

◄ **Roy Bittan**
With The E Street Band

Stevie Wonder

As well as being one of popular music's greatest singers, songwriters, and performers, Stevie Wonder also helped popularize the use of various keyboards and synthesizers.

He first hit the charts as a 12-year-old in 1962 and was originally known primarily as a singer and harmonica player. After fulfilling the terms of his initial contract with Motown in 1971 he negotiated a new deal that gave him full creative control and saw him head into evermore inventive and experimental territory. It was around the same time that he began a lengthy association with the pioneering synthesizer duo Tonto's Expanding Head Band, who played a key role in the sound of the albums he made over the next few years. *Music of My Mind* (1971) and *Talking Book* (1972) introduced a new, heavily synthesized sound and kickstarted a run of five classic albums in as many years that continued with *Innervisions* (1973), *Fulfillingness' First Finale* (1974) and the double-disc set *Songs in the Key of Life* (1976).

Wonder made use of a wide range of acoustic and electric keyboards during this phase of his career, from piano to Rhodes to Moog and beyond. Perhaps the most important of his many influential moves was his adoption of the Clavinet for such funky hits as "Superstition," which was almost single-handedly responsible for the popularisation of the instrument. He continued to experiment right through to the end of the decade when, in 1979, he released *Journey Through the Secret Life of Plants*, one of the first albums to make use of digital sampling synthesizers.

Although his music had by then become decidedly less innovative, Wonder hit his commercial peak in the 80s with the release of the chart-topping singles "Happy Birthday," "Ebony and Ivory" (a duet with Paul McCartney), and "I Just Called to Say I Love You." But while his later recordings might have had less of an influence on subsequent generations of musicians, he remains one of the most respected figures in popular music.   TJS

Ryuichi Sakamoto

A composer as much as he is a keyboardist, Sakamoto rose to international prominence during the late 70s as a member of Yellow Magic Orchestra, the synth-pop trio hailed as Japan's answer to Kraftwerk.

Born in 1952, he wrote his first piano piece at the age of four and subsequently studied composition at the University Of Tokyo before founding YMO in his mid 20s with fellow multi-instrumentalists Yukihiro Takahashi and Haruomi Hosono. Generally

▼ **Stevie Wonder**
One of the most respected men in music

◀ **Ryuichi Sakamoto**
Composer and keyboardist

jauntier and more expressive than the work of their "kosmische" forebears, the group's songs are characterized by fast synthesizer runs and taut, metronomic rhythms. All three members deploy a variety of high-tech synthesizers of the era, including Moogs, ARPs, Korgs, and a programmable Oberheim keyboard. The group's most memorable recordings include the singles "Firecracker" and "Rydeen" and the albums *Yellow Magic Orchestra* and *Solid State Survivor*.

Since leaving Yellow Magic Orchestra, Sakamoto has made a number of solo albums and collaborated with a wide range of artists including Brian Wilson, David Byrne, Thomas Dolby, and Youssou N'Dour. He has also written and recorded several movie soundtracks including *The Last Emperor* (1987), for which he won an Academy Award, and *Snake Eyes* (1998). He is perhaps best known for "Forbidden Colours," the main theme he wrote for *Merry Christmas Mr. Lawrence* (in which he also starred, alongside David Bowie and Tom Conti). The single version pits Sakamoto's gentle acoustic piano and electronic rhythms against a vocal by David Sylvian of the British group Japan, and was a minor UK hit on its release in 1982. TJS

Gary Numan

Gary Numan was born Gary Webb in London, England, in 1958. Although his name is virtually synonymous with synth-rock, he started out as a guitarist. His band, Tubeway Army, was signed to Beggars Banquet records on the strength of punk-influenced demos, and its first album was dominated by guitar-driven new wave. Things changed with the band's third single, "Down in the Park," followed by the international hit "Are 'Friends' Electric?," and the subsequent album, *The Pleasure Principle,* (all released 1979), for which Numan shed the Tubeway Army name. A track from the album, "Cars," released in 1980, was a Top 10 hit in the U.S. By now, Numan was making rock music without guitars, feeding synthesizers through effects pedals and layering the harsh, metallic tones to produce cold, dystopian music that chimed with the times.

▲ **Gary Numan**
On vocals with synth-pop pioneers
Tubeway Army

Numan is on record as saying that his Damascene conversion to synthesizers came about when he arrived at a recording studio for a session to find a Minimoog left by the previous incumbents. By simply reproducing his guitar riffs on the monophonic keyboard he created his sound and became one of the pioneers of electronic rock. This story reveals the extent to which Numan was a product of his times. By the late 1970s small, affordable synthesizers were just starting to become readily available. A few years before the idea that anyone would have left a synth lying around in a dingy budget studio would have been unthinkable, such was their rarity, value, and size. In fairness, Numan was not *just* a product of his times but an influence on them too. He became one of rock's first successful synthesizer stars, showing the world that you could make hit records with keyboards, even if you could only play them with one finger at a time.

In the 80s and 90s, Numan's career went into a decline, but with the birth of the new century he was hailed as one of the godfathers of electronic music, and his songs were much covered and sampled by a new generation of musicians. In 2008 he went on tour in the UK, during which he played Tubeway Army's 1979 album *Replicas* in full.   MB

Jools Holland

One of Britain's finest and most popular pianists and bandleaders, Jools Holland has been unfairly maligned over the years for his tendency to muscle in with the guests on his long-running BBC television series, *Later*. But there's much more to him than that.

Born in Blackheath, on the outskirts of London, in 1958, Holland first rose to prominence in the mid 70s as the teenage keyboardist in Squeeze, the new-wave pop group led by Chris Difford and Glenn Tilbrook. Many of the group's best-known songs, such as "Up the Junction" and "Cool for Cats" are underpinned by his strident piano and organ playing. Even before the group reached its peak in 1979, however,

keyboard facts

◀ **Jools Holland**
A left hand that never stops

Holland had developed an affinity for music far outside the Squeeze remit, namely boogie woogie, rhythm & blues, and jazz.

Since leaving Squeeze (first in 1981 and then in 1990, having rejoined in 1985), Holland has pursued a dual career as a musician and television presenter. As well as working on the BBC and Channel 4 in Britain he also cohosted *Sunday Night* on NBC during 1988–90. He has also recorded and toured both as a solo artist, with his Rhythm & Blues Orchestra, and in collaboration with artists such as George Harrison, Eric Clapton, Bono, and B.B. King, who later remarked: "I didn't think anybody could play like that . . . Jools has got that left hand that never stops." TJS

Vince Clarke

A founder member of Depeche Mode, Yazoo, and Erasure, Clarke is one of the most important synthesizer musicians of recent decades. He was born in Basildon, England, in 1960, and formed French Look, which eventually became Depeche Mode, in 1979 with guitarist-keyboardists Martin Gore and Andrew Fletcher. (Vocalist Dave Gahan joined a year later.) Clarke wrote the group's first three singles, "Dreaming Of Me," "New Life," and "Just Can't Get Enough," all of which have a kind of humanist Kraftwerk sound dominated by dueling melodic synth-leads. By the time the album *Speak & Spell* was released Clarke had left the group to form Yazoo ("Yaz" in the U.S.) with singer Alison Moyet, with whom he mined a similar line of upbeat electro-pop on singles such as "Only You" and "Don't Go."

After Yazoo split in 1983 Clarke formed another shortlived project, The Assembly, with producer and engineer Eric Radcliffe. By 1985, however, he had joined vocalist Andy Bell to form Erasure. It was around this time that Clarke began to use the Casio CZ-101, one of the first programmable polyphonic synths, which features on many of the duo's early releases.

Erasure reached their commercial peak in 1988 with the release of *The Innocents*, which spawned a pair of U.S. hits, "Chains Of Love" and "A Little Respect." (Both songs formed part of a run of 24 consecutive Top 20 hits in the UK.) The duo continue

Vince Clarke ▶
With Erasure vocalist Andy Bell

to record together in the 21st century, while Clarke has also worked as a solo artist and as a remixer of other acts' material.   TJS

Lisa Coleman

One of Prince's closest collaborators of the 80s, and a key member of The Revolution, Coleman played on some of the decade's biggest and most memorable hits.

The daughter of 60s session percussionist Gary Coleman, she joined Prince's backing group in 1980 at the age of 19, shortly after the release of his *Dirty Mind* album. Prince's early works were very much solo affairs, but over the next few years he allowed his backing musicians to play a more active role in songwriting and recording. By the mid 80s he had taken to sending demos of new material to Coleman and guitarist Wendy Melvoin (an old friend whom she had introduced to Prince in 1983) for the pair to flesh out with new instrumental flourishes. The duo's contributions are most prominent on *Around the World in a Day* and *Parade*, the soundtrack to *Under the Cherry Moon*.

Although her synthesizer parts are often deceptively simple, Coleman was also capable of deft, classical-style piano, as heard on tracks such as *Parade*'s "Sometimes it Snows in April," which she co-wrote. At one stage Prince planned to include her solo piano piece "Visions" on an album entitled *Dream Factory*, until he scrapped it and started work on *Sign "O" the Times* instead.

After The Revolution disbanded, Coleman and Melvoin struck out on their own, first as Wendy and Lisa and later as The Girl Bros. They have also played with and produced acts including Sheryl Crow, Liz Phair, and Seal, and recorded a number of television and movie soundtracks.   TJS

keyboard facts

Tori Amos

The first of a long line of female singer-songwriters to emerge during the 90s, Amos is also an accomplished pianist and multi-instrumentalist. Born in 1963, Amos reportedly started playing the piano at age of two; by five she had become the youngest ever student at the Peabody Conservatory of Music. By the late 70s, having been expelled from the school at 11, she was playing regularly in piano bars in and around Maryland and Washington D.C. She cut her debut solo album in 1991 after a brief period fronting the much-maligned Y Kant Tori Read. *Little Earthquakes* set her richly melodic, expressive playing against a series of complex, idiosyncratic songs often reminiscent of Kate Bush.

Over the next few years Amos continued to develop both as a songwriter and as a musician. After making another largely piano-based album, *Under the Pink* (featuring the hit "Cornflake Girl") in 1994, she expanded her musical palette considerably for 1996's *Boys for Pele*, on which she plays harmonium, harpsichord, and clavichord. On subsequent tours in support of the albums *From the Choirgirl Hotel* and *Scarlet's Walk* she added Fender Rhodes, Wurlitzer, and several Kurzweil synthesizers to her arsenal of keyboard instruments. Perhaps the most striking change to her playing style, however, came with the album *The Beekeeper* (2005), which she recorded after being given a Hammond B-3 for her birthday, and which has a much more rhythmic, textural feel than previous efforts. The change seemed consistent with the release of the five-disc retrospective *A Piano* a year later, which Amos claimed would mark the end of an era and the start of a move toward a more rock-based sound. TJS

Rob Collins

During the 90s, it seemed to become less and less common for bands to include a permanent keyboard player. One prominent exception, however, was the British group The Charlatans, whose sound was often dominated—until his sudden death in 1996—by the playing of organist Rob Collins.

Collins was born in 1965 and cofounded The Charlatans in 1990. His rhythmic organ playing gave the group something that set them apart from their contemporaries in the late 80s/early 90s "baggy" scene, which was spearheaded by The Stones Roses and The Happy Mondays. His stop-start Hammond is at the forefront of the group's debut hit, "The Only One I Know," which reached the UK Top 10 in 1990, as well as

▼ **Lisa Coleman**
With Wendy Melvoin in Wendy and Lisa

▲ **Tori Amos**
Singer, songwriter, multi-instrumentalist

other early highlights such as the spy-movie-evoking "Weirdo" and the funky, electric piano-led "Tremelo Song."

The Charlatans fell out of favor somewhat over the next couple of years—a situation not helped by Collins's brief imprisonment for his role in an armed robbery—but returned to prominence in 1994 with an eponymous fourth album. Collins is at center stage once more on *The Charlatans*, on which he plays various electric and acoustic pianos, Mellotron, and Clavinet as well as his usual Hammond. He and the rest of the group seemed to be approaching the peak of their powers until disaster struck midway through sessions for their fifth album, *Tellin' Stories*, during the summer of 1996, when Collins was killed in a road accident. The remaining Charlatans brought in Primal Scream keyboardist Martin Duffy to help complete the album, but Collins still features on most of the tracks. The powerful, piano-led "One to Another," released five weeks after his death, serves as a fitting epitaph for his work with the group.   TJS

Money Mark

Although not particularly well known in his own right, Mark Ramos-Nishita is notable for his work during the 90s and early 21st century with alternative acts such as The Beastie Boys and Beck. Through his solo work, he also helped rekindle an interest in vintage synths and keyboards at a time when such instruments seemed to have become something to be used rather than played.

Nishita met The Beastie Boys by chance in the early 90s while working as a handyman. It just so happened that the group was in the midst of moving away from making music with programmed beats and samples to working with real instruments, and needed a keyboardist. As Money Mark, Nishita played an integral role in the making of the group's next two albums, *Check Your Head* (1992) and *Ill Communication*

keyboard facts

(1994). His funky organ and electric piano can be heard throughout both albums on tracks such as "Sure Shot," "Something's Got To Give," and "Groove Holmes."

Over the next few years Nishita became a much sought-after session player, appearing on albums by The Wallflowers, Cornelius, Ben Lee, and The Jon Spencer Blues Explosion. His most memorable guest appearance came in 1996, when he played the funky, Doors-like electric-piano part that underpins Beck's international hit "Where It's At." It followed the release of his full-length solo debut, *Mark's Keyboard Repair*, on which he plays a range of vintage synths and keyboards, making particularly prominent use of his beloved MicroMoog. Nishita has made several more well-received albums in the years since, including *Push The Button* (1998) and *Brand New By Tomorrow* (2007), and continues to work with The Beastie Boys and other acts. TJS

Jonny Greenwood

Although generally thought of, first and foremost, as a guitarist, Radiohead's Jonny Greenwood (born 1971) is equally at home behind a keyboard as he is plugged into a guitar amp.

After restricting himself mostly to guitar on Radiohead's early work, Greenwood had begun to take wider steps away from the six-string by the time of 1997's landmark *OK Computer*. "Karma Police" is underpinned by his stately, Beatles-esque piano chords, while he plays a Moog on several other tracks. (The album does of course also showcase some of his most expressive and innovative guitar-playing.)

By the time of *Kid A* (2000) and *Amnesiac* (2001), Greenwood had expanded his arsenal of keyboards to include the Ondes Martenot, an early electronic instrument that can be played by sliding a metal ring along a ribbon to produce a sound similar to that of a Theremin. It can be heard most prominently on songs such as "The National Anthem" and "How To Disappear Completely."

Greenwood has also written classical pieces for the martenot, and used it in his soundtracks to the films *Bodysong* and *There Will Be Blood*. His bandmate Thom Yorke, meanwhile, has also moved away from the guitar as Radiohead's career has progressed. Many of Radiohead's best songs are driven by his stark, unconventional playing on either acoustic piano ("Pyramid Song" and "Videotape") or Fender Rhodes ("Everything in its Right Place" and "Morning Bell"). TJS

▲ **Money Mark**
With The Beastie Boys

Mikael Jorgensen

As the principal keyboardist in the current incarnation of Wilco, Mikael Jorgensen has established himself as an unfussy yet integral addition to the alternative rock group's line-up. Having worked previously as a DJ and producer, Jorgensen joined Wilco for the tour in support of the group's acclaimed fourth album, *Yankee Hotel Foxtrot*. His role was initially to trigger samples and perform real-time sound manipulations from the side of the stage, but it quickly became apparent to frontman Jeff Tweedy that he was capable of "a lot more than we were using him for."

Jorgensen became a full-time member of the group prior to the recording of *A Ghost Is Born*, on which he plays piano and keyboards. His deft playing underpins tracks such as "Hell is Chrome" and "Theologians" (both of which he cowrote), and serves generally to widen the group's sonic palette throughout. As well as traditional keyboard instruments, he also plays an RMI Rocksichord—an early-60s synthesized approximation of a harpsichord—on several tracks, and a stylophone on "Company on My Back."

Jorgensen plays a similarly subtle but effective role on the follow-up, 2007's *Sky Blue Sky*. His gentle flourishes of piano and organ offer a fine example of how best to integrate electric and acoustic keyboards into a full-band sound on standout tracks such as "Either Way," "Side with the Seeds," and "Shake it Off." In a live setting, meanwhile, his piano is often augmented by the additional keyboards played by multi-instrumentalist Pat Sansone, lending the group a sound reminiscent of The Band. TJS

Jonny Greenwood
Going beyond guitar with Radiohead

▼ **Mikael Jorgensen (right)**
With the acclaimed Wilco

2 the history

Jerry Lee Lewis
Faithful to the piano throughout his career

▲ **Playing the spinet**
This 18th-century painting shows Christina Antonio Somis at the keyboard of a small spinet, accompanied by other members of her family on cello and violin.

▼ **Virginals**
A lavishly decorated virginals, made in Italy in the 1660s.

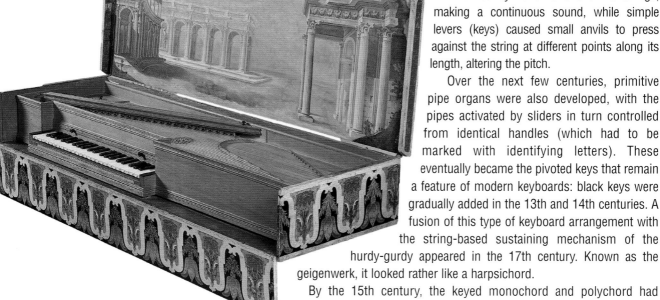

The Piano Story
By Carl Humphries

It is tempting to see the 1,000-year history of acoustic keyboards as a process of evolution, with the modern piano as its end result. Certainly the piano is more important than any other keyboard instrument in most types of music today.

Like other keyboard instruments (such as harpsichords and organs), the piano allows an individual player to create melody, harmony, and texture all at once, unfolding the complex structures of western music in the process. At the same time, the piano retains a large element of the physically expressive control over sound that is natural to singing and playing but missing from other keyboard instruments.

This combination of factors has enabled the piano to become the central instrument of western music, both for virtuoso performers, composers, and improvisers, and for ordinary people making music in their own homes, where it remains easily the most mechanically complex piece of equipment to be found.

The piano uses small hammers that strike the strings inside and bounce off, leaving the strings to vibrate freely. This mechanism has its origins in early forms of zither—an instrument that back to the Bronze Age—in which strings stretched between sticks or over a wooden board are struck or plucked. Later the zither developed considerably, thanks to the addition of a resonating chamber and moveable bridges that could alter the pitch of the note, as on the monochords used by ancient Greeks in their early experiments with the mathematics of musical tuning and harmony. Sophisticated examples of zither still in use include the Japanese koto and Hungarian cimbalom.

The first zithers arrived in Europe from the Middle East in the 11th century, as portable instruments (psalteries). From these the dulcimer evolved, the first such instrument with metal strings specifically designed to be struck by small hammers. The dulcimer became an important precursor of the expressive control over volume offered by the modern piano. Taken up and developed in the late 17th century by Pantaleon Hebenstreit, a virtuosic German player, the dulcimer showed the exciting possibilities of having a struck stringed instrument where volume could be freely and dramatically varied.

Although the Greeks and Romans are thought to have used a primitive form of water-organ that operated rather like a keyboard, the hurdy-gurdy (or organistrum) was probably the first stringed instrument to use a keyboard, appearing around the 10th century. This used a wheel that was turned by hand to stroke the strings, making a continuous sound, while simple levers (keys) caused small anvils to press against the string at different points along its length, altering the pitch.

Over the next few centuries, primitive pipe organs were also developed, with the pipes activated by sliders in turn controlled from identical handles (which had to be marked with identifying letters). These eventually became the pivoted keys that remain a feature of modern keyboards: black keys were gradually added in the 13th and 14th centuries. A fusion of this type of keyboard arrangement with the string-based sustaining mechanism of the hurdy-gurdy appeared in the 17th century. Known as the geigenwerk, it looked rather like a harpsichord.

By the 15th century, the keyed monochord and polychord had

appeared, and it was from the latter that the clavichord most probably evolved. The clavichord produces sound by striking the strings from beneath with small metal hammers known as tangents. At the same time as setting the strings vibrating, the hammers "stop" the string and hence determine its pitch. The process is akin to that of a violinist or guitarist using the left hand to alter the length of a string to produce the required note. In the case of the clavichord, the tangent divides the string into two lengths; one which is permanently damped by felt, the other which vibrates and provides the note.

The compass of the keyboard on this and other keyboard instruments was significantly expanded during the 16th century, from two octaves to four-and-a-half. This process continued with the development of harpsichords, and then pianos, through to six-octave instruments at the end of the 18th century. The modern piano keyboard has a compass of 88 notes, covering a little over seven octaves.

Alongside the clavichord, whose existence was first reported in 1404, there emerged a family of keyboard instruments with mechanically plucked strings: the harpsichord, virginals, and spinet. These used a sophisticated mechanism (the jack) to pluck the strings and then damp them when the key was released. They differ from one another in shape, size, and arrangement of strings.

The clavichord, spinet, and virginals, though extremely popular, were too quiet to be effective outside of small domestic gatherings. By contrast the harpsichord was expanded to produce a bigger sound, with the strings running perpendicular to the keyboard (in the same direction as the keys) and with several strings for each note, sometimes tuned to different octaves.

Stops were introduced to create a crude sense of dynamic contrast, either by lifting all the dampers away from the strings at once (producing more resonance through sympathetic vibration of strings) or by keeping them partially in contact with the strings as the notes sounded.

In spite of its popularity and suitability for concert use throughout the 17th and 18th centuries, the harpsichord could not provide the dynamic control of individual notes illustrated by the dulcimer or even the clavichord. That meant demand for a concert keyboard instrument with real dynamic control remained unsatisfied, paving the way for the introduction of the piano.

Harpsichord ▲
A replica of a 1638 Ruckers double-manual harpsichord. Extra keyboards, or "manuals," were added to some harpsichords from the 17th century.

Bartolomeo Cristofori's great invention

By the end of the 17th century, three types of keyboard instrument were in use: organs, the harpsichord family, and clavichords. None offered the sort of dynamic response that would allow keyboard players to achieve the subtle expressive contrasts of volume being demonstrated by other performers, such as violinists and string orchestras.

The first instruments recognizable today as pianos were built by Bartolomeo Cristofori, the keeper of instruments at the Florentine court, at the turn of the 18th century. He built only

Cristofori piano ▲
Built in Florence, Italy, in 1722.

the piano story

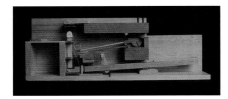
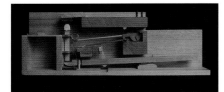
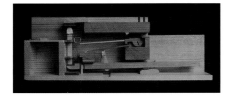
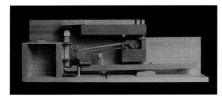
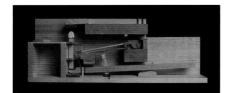

▲ **Cristofori's action**
This sequence of pictures illustrates the action of Cristofori's 1726 piano.

a small number of pianos, but brilliantly solved the technical problems posed by an instrument in which strings have to be struck by hammers. But his results were practically ignored by the musicians of his own time in Italy.

A visitor to Cristofori described the resulting instrument as a "gravicembalo col piano e forte" (a harpsichord with soft and loud), and it is from this that the modern piano takes its name. (Piano is short for pianoforte: some early instruments are known as fortepianos.) In spite of the lack of interest, Cristofori continued to refine his piano action, even developing the *una corda* mechanism that corresponds to the left-hand pedal on modern pianos. He used a hand stop to direct the hammer at just one of the two strings used for each note. He also discovered that longer, thicker strings would produce more tone, providing that the strings could be securely maintained under a greater tension. That meant strengthening the case and altering the way the tuning pins were mounted in the wooden block that supported them.

Cristofori's greatest stroke of genius was his development of the escapement mechanism, whereby the single downward movement of the key is converted into two distinct movements of the hammer: upwards to hit the string, then immediately back down again so that the string is left free to vibrate. The trick was to let the hammer (and its shank) "escape" from the rest of the mechanism, so that it was free to rebound and fall back down (with gravity) on hitting the string, even if the piano key remained depressed. It was no longer connected to the part of the piano mechanism controlled by the keys.

In terms of tonal character, the pianos of Cristofori bear little resemblance to the instruments of today. The sound is much more delicate and projects less than that of the harpsichord, and the touch is extremely light, owing to the small size of the hammers. Nevertheless, they do achieve a real dynamic range while being considerably more powerful than the clavichord.

The action moves to London

In the early decades of the 18th century a number of instrument manufacturers in France and Germany, inspired by the success of Hebenstreit and working independently of Cristofori, experimented with actions that used hammers to strike strings. None of these really took off until Gottfried Silbermann came across a description of Cristofori's instruments and attempted to recreate their design, developing his own version of the piano action, known as *Prellmechanik*.

In 1736 Silbermann showed his instruments to the greatest German composer of the time, Johann Sebastian Bach, who was impressed but stated that the action was heavy and the upper register weak. After many years of refinement Silbermann once

Beyer square piano ▶
Built in London in 1777 by Adam Beyer.

keyboard facts

again presented one of his pianos, this time in Potsdam at the court of Frederick the Great (King Frederick II of Prussia), a keen music enthusiast and amateur composer. This time the instrument was acclaimed.

It is probably no coincidence that the court composer in Potsdam for many years was Carl Phillip Emmanuel Bach, the most original composer among the elder Bach's numerous sons, and the one who did more than anyone else to found the modern school of keyboard playing. C.P.E. Bach's intensely dramatic, emotionally involved, and highly adventurous approach to keyboard composing and extemporizing reflected the new penchant for emotionalism (*Empfindsamkeit*) in German culture. Although his music was probably principally conceived for the harpsichord, it laid the foundations for the pianistic styles of Mozart, Haydn, and Beethoven, as well as for the subsequent role of the piano as the instrument on which composing and improvising most fully overlap and interact. It retained this role throughout the 19th century and, through jazz, into the 20th century.

Silbermann's *Prellmechanik* action was taken up and developed by Johann Andreas Stein, who added his own escapement (*zunge*) to produce the *Prellzungenmechanik* or "German action." This became popular with German manufacturers and was later modified (with the addition of a check mechanism) to become the Viennese action in pianos used by many of the great composers of the classical period, such as Mozart and Haydn. By contrast, Cristofori's later action (which came to be known as *Stosszungemechanik*) influenced the "English action" (known in its earliest pre-escapement forms simply as *Stossmechanik*) to form the basis of subsequent developments in English piano design.

The Seven Years War, which broke out in Germany in 1756, drove many piano manufacturers to England, including Americus Backers and Johannes Zumpe, who both sought to develop the possibilities of Cristofori's action. Zumpe developed a square piano with a simplified action (without an escapement) that could be built easily at a lower cost than harpsichords. It was soon in huge demand in London, especially after J.C. Bach gave the first acclaimed public recital on the instrument in London, featuring his own works, probably the first to be composed specifically for the instrument. Zumpe marketed his instrument effectively, aiming it at the middle classes rather than the aristocracy, and keeping the casework simple with this in mind. Later models of square piano tended to be more ornate, however.

John Broadwood also began to build square pianos around the 1770s, and quickly produced an enhanced version, featuring underdamping (dampers below rather than above the strings) and a sustaining pedal: two important distinguishing features of the modern piano. However, as the demand grew for more tonal power and projection, it became necessary to increase the length and tension of the strings. This eventually forced Broadwood to develop an iron hitch pin plate that could be installed above the soundboard. By 1821 his firm had built the first square piano with such a feature.

However, it was the grand piano that emerged as the principal concert instrument as the 19th century progressed. At the same time, the increasing size of the square piano eventually led to its replacement as a domestic instrument by the upright, since people wanted smaller instruments for their homes.

▼ **Hand-stops**
The Beyer piano (opposite) included brass hand-stops for damping effects.

Power and sweetness

Vienna dominated the musical life of Europe from the late 18th century through to the early decades of the 19th century. The ruling Habsburgs were enthusiastic patrons of the arts, including music, and so artists and those with related skills were drawn to the city. Vienna became another focus for the piano industry, like London, but the sort of instruments that emerged in the two cities were quite different, as they rested on contrasting types of action: the "Viennese" action and the "English" action.

Like London, Vienna attracted a number of German piano makers, and many of these adopted Stein's improved escapement action (*Prellzungenmechanik*), in which

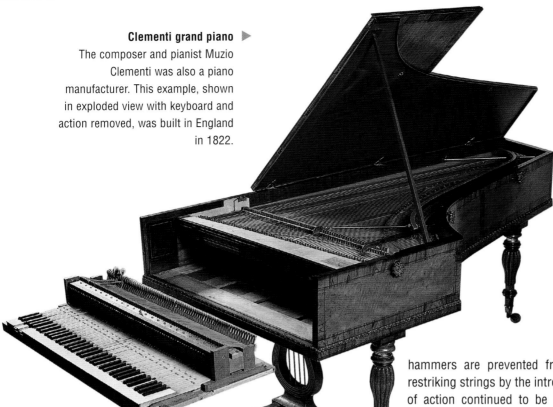

Clementi grand piano ▶
The composer and pianist Muzio Clementi was also a piano manufacturer. This example, shown in exploded view with keyboard and action removed, was built in England in 1822.

hammers are prevented from bouncing back up and restriking strings by the introduction of checks. This type of action continued to be used by numerous German makers right up to the start of the 20th century.

The sound of these Viennese grand pianos is much lighter and more delicate than that of modern instruments, and this can sometimes shed light on the musical intentions of the great Viennese composers such as Mozart, Haydn, and Beethoven. By the 1780s, the English and Viennese grand pianos had become quite distinct as instruments. The former has a lighter construction and is normally double-strung. The latter is usually triple-strung and has a heavier construction. The Viennese action is also lighter, while the English action is more complex, with the hammers mounted on a separate hammer rail.

Unlike the more powerful English instruments, whose hammers strike the strings in a direct manner, the hammers of the Viennese instruments tend almost to caress the strings as they hit them, producing a gentler and sweeter sound. But unlike the English pianos, these instruments were constructed in such a way that it was impossible to adapt them to satisfy the ever-increasing demand for more volume, without sacrificing the responsiveness of the action. This eventually led them to fall out of favor as increasing numbers of players preferred to use the English and French models.

At the same time as this shift occurred, the center of attention of musical culture in Europe was moving from Vienna to Paris.

In England the success of the square piano during the late 1760s had led to an especially strong demand for an instrument with a richer tone and greater dynamic response. The new action that was to facilitate this was developed by Backus, in conjunction with Broadwood and Stodart, on the basis of the designs of Cristofori and Silbermann. Here, pianos were already big business, causing Clementi, the leading piano composer and pianist of the day in London, to go into business as a manufacturer as well. The manufacturing process became geared to factory mass-production much more rapidly in Britain than elsewhere.

John Broadwood went further and engaged the assistance of scientific experts to help him improve the technical consistency of his designs. As a result he altered the point at which the string is struck, to improve the quality of tone. He also divided the bridge into two sections. These modifications enabled him to add half an octave at the top and bottom of his grand pianos.

keyboard facts

Such was the success of these improvements that the aging and deaf Beethoven expressed his delight on being presented with a Broadwood grand. He believed it to be the only instrument remotely capable of fulfilling the taxing demands of his increasingly dramatic and extreme compositions.

Piano and the Romantics

The French Revolution led to several major piano makers in France leaving to set up factories in England. One of the most important was Sébastien Erard, who spotted that the market was shifting away from the square piano and so focused on the grand piano.

Erard's most important innovation was the double escapement mechanism, which allows a note to be replayed without the key having to be fully released, permitting much speedier note repetition. English makers doubted the durability of this complex mechanism, and made the mistake of ignoring it for several decades.

The 19th century was the period in which the Romantic movement emerged in European classical music, leading to an emphasis on emotional intensity and drama in both works and performances. Audiences liked to see musicians transported into states of poetic and emotional rapture, and many concerts ended with wrecked pianos. In fact it was usually the strings, rather than the action, that presented the problem: their thickness (and thus their strength) was constrained by the limited tension that the framework of the instrument could support without warping. Thicker, stronger strings could be used, but to reach the same pitches as thinner strings they had to be put under higher tension, and that meant building a stronger framework.

Manufacturers began to use iron spacers between the pin block and the belly rail to which the hitch-pin plate is itself fixed, but even these could bend under pressure. The solution was to attach iron braces running above the soundboard, on the same plane as the strings, and fixed to the hitch-pin plate. Broadwood and Erard both lay claim to this development. Eventually the number of braces was reduced, owing to the advent of more efficient fixings capable of withstanding greater forces. With the increase in string tension, larger hammers and more robust actions became feasible. Steinway would achieve the other important advances paving the way for the modern grand piano in the mid-19th century, with the introduction of the full-iron frame (originally patented by Chickering) and the development of overstringing.

The musical consequences of these developments were enormous. The increased dynamic range over a much wider compass, along with the sustaining pedal, allowed romantic composer-performers such as Chopin, Schumann, and Liszt to explore an unprecedented variety of new moods and textures, as well as performing technical fireworks that would previously have been unthinkable. The piano became the centerpiece of Romantic soirées, in which the great names of the day would entrance audiences with their displays of emotion and dazzling virtuosity.

Like the lean and otherworldly Paganini, a violinist whom many believed to be the devil in disguise, Liszt encouraged the public to see him as a demonically talented individual. He would often improvise extravagantly on his own and other people's compositions. Like Schumann, he exploited the piano's unique ability to evoke the complex and sensual images of Romantic literature through its rich variety of textures.

Meanwhile, the exiled Polish composer-virtuoso Chopin captured the hearts of audiences with the soulful melancholy and haunting sensuality of his piano compositions, still felt by many to encapsulate the innermost soul of the instrument. It is interesting to note that Chopin, together with some other performers of the day, preferred the tonal subtlety of Pleyel instruments to the mechanical sophistication of Erards, but also played Broadwoods in England. As late as the end of the 19th century, a few late-Romantic composers, notably Mahler, still preferred the old Viennese-style piano with its associations of old Vienna and the great classical masters.

▼ **Erard grand piano**
Built by the Erard brothers in 1808 for King Louis of the Netherlands.

▲ **Clara Schumann (left)**
The leading female virtuoso of the day, who also taught many great players.

Kirkman grand piano ▷
Made in London in 1820, this piano was allegedly owned by King George IV and kept at Brighton Pavilion in England.

This period also saw the foundation of the first great European school of piano playing. The brilliant composer Robert Schumann married the leading female virtuoso of the day, Clara Wieck. Her father was a leading piano teacher who had groomed her from birth for an international career. Clara Schumann, as she became known, taught many of great pianists, whose influence continued to be felt through into the 20th century, and her own performances of works by others were often proceeded by improvised preludes of her own invention. Her own compositional talents were sadly eclipsed by her husband's career, but she encouraged her students to improvise around the pieces of music they were learning in order to gain a better understanding of them, a method recently revived by some of the most progressive classical teachers of the present day.

The evolution of the upright

The upright we know today first appeared around 1800, following previous attempts to design vertical grand pianos (known as upright grands). It was developed to be a smaller, more economical and portable instrument. However, manufacturers also wanted an instrument whose sound retained as many as possible of the qualities of the grand piano.

More than one designer had independently realized that the legs of the upright grand were redundant, so the bass strings could go right to the floor. Shortly after that, Thomas Loud of London proposed running the strings diagonally, so that either longer strings could be incorporated or the size of the case could be reduced. Loud went to America, where he produced small pianos, while in Europe obliquely strung pianos of this kind became known as pianinos.

Another Londoner, William Southwell, had introduced the sticker action in 1798, which allowed the hammer to be positioned at the optimum point on the strings, adding an escapement and a check, but it was Robert Wornum who transformed the upright piano into the instrument we know today. Early on, Wornum built an upright that combined diagonal stringing with the English double action, and in the 1830s he went on to develop the tape-check action that remains the basis for the system used in uprights today. It employs a piece of tape to check the hammer so that it cannot strike more than once. In 1842 he patented his most advanced version of this action, and his innovation was further developed in Paris by Pleyel and Pape, so that it became known, wrongly, as the "French" action. The French manufacturers of uprights were commercially successful, but in mass production to meet demand, artistic standards may have suffered.

The upright piano was a product that could be sold to the middle classes, but it also had the prestige of having evolved from the grand pianos of the wealthier and more aristocratic parts of society. Size was an extremely important issue, since the typical middle-class home in the mid 19th century had smallish rooms. The upright piano was often adapted or disguised to function as something else when not in use. Pianos could resemble tables and desks, or even chests of drawers. English and French manufacturers were especially inventive in enhancing the domestic appeal of the instrument, and the designs of Pape, though expensive, inspired other makers to experiment.

The evolution of the modern grand

The great exhibitions and world fairs of the 19th century offered excellent opportunities for the major piano manufacturers to present their new designs to the public. As a result, American piano makers, led by Steinway and Chickering, made a huge impact in the European market in the second half of the 19th century. They won many awards at major exhibitions with their advanced production techniques and new ideas for design and marketing.

The Steinway family (originally called Steinweg) had immigrated to America after the 1848 revolution in Germany, where they had already been producing pianos. They produced a series of innovations in the production and design process: these represent the last major developments in the evolution of the modern grand piano.

In the 1850s they introduced overstringing to square pianos, and developed a cast-iron frame that could support far greater levels of tension in the strings, making it possible to produce instruments with a much bigger and richer sound. By 1860, they had produced the overstrung grand—the real forerunner of the modern concert grand—and had began to make use of a process for machine-felting their hammers to achieve a more consistent tonal quality.

Theodor Steinway, the only member of the family to have remained behind in Germany in the 1850s, worked closely with the great 19th-century German scientist and acoustician Hermann Helmholtz, who had investigated the acoustic foundations of musical instruments and musical harmony. After moving to America in the 1860s, Theodor Steinway introduced a whole series of technical refinements that were eventually taken up by other manufacturers around the world, notably the single-piece laminated piano rim.

During World War II the American factory of Steinway & Sons was used to make aircraft parts, while the German factory was taken over by the Nazis to produce dummy aeroplanes and rifle butts. The Steinway firm acquired the reputation as the world's premiere piano maker, partly through developing close relationships with international concert artists, many of whom were inclined to refuse to perform on any other kind of piano.

Apart from Broadwood & Sons and Steinway & Sons, the 19th century saw the emergence of a number of other great piano firms, three of which stand out for the quality of their instruments. Bösendorfer of Vienna and Bechstein of Berlin both prided themselves on creating instruments capable of surviving the ferocious onslaught of Liszt's piano playing. Bösendorfer supplied instruments to the Austrian Imperial Court, and remains the leading Austrian piano firm, also creating an instrument with additional notes at the very bottom that extended the range down to low C below the A that is normally the lowest note on modern pianos. Bechstein skillfully integrated the best of the many other developments in piano manufacture into their grand pianos.

The Leipzig-based firm of Julius Blüthner was admired for the tonal beauty of its

▲ Racca Piano Melodico
This "melody piano" was built by Giovanni Racca in Bologna, Italy, around 1900. An improvement over the barrel piano, it allowed longer tunes to be played by using folded cardboard sheets and a crank-operated mechanism.

instruments, particularly in the late 19th century and early 20th century, and production was revived after World War II under the auspices of the East German government. Blüthner made an important innovation in the form of the "aliquot" system, in which an extra string is added for each note in the higher register for sympathetic vibration, to enhance the singing quality of the tone.

Mechanized pianos

The popularity of the piano prompted manufacturers to try to think of ways to bring the instrument into homes where no one could actually play it. The obvious solution was to mechanize the instrument.

Mechanical instruments such as music boxes had been popular in Europe since the 14th century, and Mozart even wrote music specifically for them. The earliest system was the "barrel" mechanism; a cylinder turned, and nails inserted into it would trigger a lever that then caused a note to sound (or the nails would themselves pluck notes on strings). The circular shape of the cylinder meant that the music automatically returned to the beginning and started again. In the 19th century, manufacturers began to fit barrel mechanisms to their pianos, but with the exception of the street piano, barrel pianos had little commercial success.

This sort of solid barrel had many limitations. For an automatic instrument to gain wide appeal a more sophisticated way of storing music was required. The solution was to use a cylinder with punched holes instead of raised nails, and the first successful automatic piano based on this idea was produced by Giovanni Racca.

▲ Tomasso street piano
This "barrel" piano was built in London in about 1885. It could play 10 tunes.

keyboard facts

In the 1880s he patented a Piano Melodico that used folded cardboard for storage.

In the 1860s a Frenchman, Fourneaux, developed a "piano player" or "Pianista," a freestanding machine that could be wheeled up to the piano so that its mechanical "fingers" played the keys. By contrast the term "player piano" refers to an instrument with an automatic player mechanism already fitted inside it. The advent of the piano roll in the 1870s made both types of automatic piano viable, since it offered a compact and efficient way of storing information about the pieces of music to be played.

Most early piano rolls were lacking in expression or dynamics, but tempo, volume and pedaling could sometimes be adjusted in a crude way by an operator. Consequently, piano players and player pianos couldn't really reproduce an actual performance by a performer. This possibility became available with the development of "reproducing pianos" in the early 20th century.

▲ **Steck reproducing piano**
The Aeolian Duo-Art piano roll system of 1912 was incorporated into Steck pianos, built in New York.

Moreover, in 1904 Edwin Welte of Freiburg in Germany invented a system for encoding every nuance of a pianist's performance, including tempo changes, dynamics, and pedaling. He also introduced an electric motor to drive the mechanism instead of pedaled bellows.

The automated piano was the jukebox of its day. But the arrival of the gramophone, and eventually the jukebox itself, led to its inevitable and swift decline. Nevertheless, its creative use later, by individuals such as the American composer Conlon Nancarrow, can be regarded as anticipating the use of modern computer sequencing techniques. Automated pianos were popular in cinemas, and this was part of a broader drive to exploit the popularity of the instrument by adapting it to as many social purposes and situations as possible. Pianos were adapted for use on yachts, and even in the ill-fated airships.

The development of electric pianos, in which the sound is electrically altered, and then of electronic pianos, in which the sound is electronically generated, produced alternative sound characteristics that were readily exploited by popular musicians. Of the former, the Fender Rhodes achieved success and significance in popular culture thanks to its distinctive sound.

In recent decades, the musical instrument industry has seized upon computer technology and digital circuitry to develop increasingly sophisticated electronic keyboards, capable of exploring a wide range of synthetic sounds or simulating the sound of an acoustic piano. The advent of MIDI means that sound can now be processed entirely in the digital domain, as just another kind of numerical data. Acoustic pianos have also been fitted with MIDI technology, allowing them to store information about an actual performance on the instrument and then replay it "for real" in the absence of the player.

Ironically, even the most sophisticated "touch-sensitive" electronic keyboard technology has not yet succeeded in matching the extraordinary sensitivity to human touch of an ordinary piano action; one of the features whose expressive importance prompted the invention of the piano in the first place.

▲ **Piano roll**
Piano rolls, invented by Edwin Welte in Germany in 1887, quickly became popular. Many great pianists made rolls for sale by Aeolian and other companies.

The modern grand

The Steinway Model D concert grand piano is the instrument used by most modern concert pianists for performance purposes. The first version of this model appeared

in 1857, although it was only after another 10 years that Steinway developed their unique technique for manufacturing the entire rim from a single piece of wood, a feature that contributes to the instrument's unique sound.

Steinway traditionally produced about 150 Model Ds each year in Hamburg (Germany) and New York (U.S.), with slight differences between the instruments originating in the two countries, since some raw materials have a different source. At the same time, it is normal for pianos of this caliber to be adjusted to suit the individual player, in order to ensure that both the tone and the responsiveness of the action are optimally suited to the individual user's musical preferences and way of playing.

Some players like to express a preference for Steinways made in the inter-war period (the 1920s and 1930s), which are felt to have a slightly darker, more introverted expressive tonal character. This may well be a reaction to the tendency to brighten the tone of modern grand pianos generally, to bring them into line with the preferences of the recording industry and of a modern concert-going public whose expectations are often influenced by what they hear on modern recordings. This characteristic is most pronounced in Far Eastern pianos (eg, Yamaha, Kawai). In other respects, however, such as the responsiveness of the piano action, these have now started to rival the subtlety that was once the sole province of the great European firms.

Tonal purists may even go out of their way to obtain one of old "patent action" Blüthner grands—instruments known for their exceptionally subtlety and beauty of tone—possibly with a view to having it reconditioned. These pianos were built at a time when the manufacturer was using a more primitive type of action, now considered inadequate and rather unreliable. However, for those who value tonal beauty above all else, or who make only modest technical demands of the instrument, this can represent an interesting choice.

▲ **Modern grand action**
The sequence illustrates the action of a Steinway grand piano.

▲ **Modern grand piano**
The Steinway Model D, shown in exploded view. It is the instrument prefered by most concert pianists.

keyboard facts

▲ Modern upright piano
The Bösendorfer Model 130, shown in exploded view, revealing frame, action, keyboard, and strings.

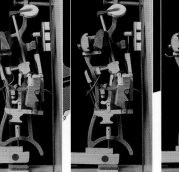
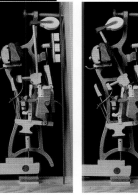

The modern upright

Modern-day teachers and performers who require a top-quality instrument at a price that does not preclude home use have often favored Bösendorfer pianos. Their Model 130 Studio is one of the most highly regarded of modern upright pianos. Most of this instrument is hand-crafted, and it takes almost a year to produce. The challenge for a manufacturer of uprights is to compensate for the effect on tonal range and projection of the inevitably shorter string lengths, and for the fact that the action requires a shorter key, which consequently offers a diminished level of responsiveness.

The height of the Model 130 Studio is typical of modern full-size uprights: about 51 inches. However, there is a range of smaller sizes available, known in the U.S. by different names, depending on their height. A "spinet" piano usually measures about 36-38 inches high, while a "console" piano is about 38-43 inches. Above this are "standard" uprights, known in Britain as "full-size" uprights. Some Americans also like to refer to instruments of 43-47 inches as "studio" pianos. The smaller types may incorporate some alterations to the action, notably the use of a "drop" action.

▲ Modern upright action
This sequence illustrates the action of the Bösendorfer Model 130.

Ondes Martenot control panel
The controls of the Ondes Martenot are idiosyncratic but highly expressive.

Ondes Martenot ▶
The keyboard of the Ondes Martenot and the different types of loudspeaker cabinet that modify its sound.

The Electronic Keyboard Story
By Gordon Reid

1870–1929

Many huge, strange, and technologically amazing keyboard instruments were developed in the latter days of the 19th century. Names such as The Musical Telegraph (US, 1876) and The Singing Arc (UK, 1899) are hugely evocative, but the instruments themselves are now long lost.

Perhaps the earliest electrical instrument still remembered today was Melvin Severy's Choralcelo (USA, 1909) which was developed over two decades from 1888–1908. Around 100 units were built, and some continued to be used until the 1950s. Like its contemporary, Thaddeus Cahill's immense Telharmonium (USA, 1906) it featured a tonewheel generator (non-circular metal discs spinning in a magnetic field to generate a waveform) but combined this with a set of piano strings that could be hit with hammers or vibrated using electromagnets. The sound then passed through filters—or, to be precise, bits of wood, glass, cardboard, metal, and even springs—to modify its tone. Unfortunately, the main body of the Choralcelo filled the basement of a substantial building, so it was never going to be possible to buy one and stick it in your living room.

The first electrical instrument to become widely available was the Aetherphon, Thereminvox, or Theremin (USSR, 1917), as it became known. This introduced an oscillator technology that would be used on numerous keyboards throughout the first half of the century, but it was a unique instrument because it was played without touching it. Instead, the player moved his (or her) hands in the vicinity of two antennas; one of which controlled the pitch of the sound, while the other controlled the loudness. Although invented in the USSR, the Theremin was patented in the USA after its inventor, Leon Termin, moved there in 1927. This exposed it to a far wider audience and, in the 1950s, it was adopted as the instrument of choice for sci-fi movie

keyboard facts

soundtracks. Still manufactured in many forms, the Theremin is extremely difficult to master, and only two players have ever been considered true virtuosi: Clara Rockmore, and Lydia Kavina, the granddaughter of Leon Termin's cousin. Nevertheless, Theremins still pop up in the unlikeliest of places.

The next significant advance was the invention of the Ondes Martenot (France, 1928) by Maurice Martenot. Like the Theremin, this produced simple waveforms, but rather than moving your hands in the air, you controlled it using an amplitude button called the Touche and a ribbon with a ring, through which you inserted a finger. Skilled Ondes Martenot players could create remarkable imitations of instruments such as violins and cellos, moving the ring along the fretless fingerboard to determine the pitch, and using the Touche to articulate notes in a realistic fashion. Like the Theremin, a version of the Ondes Martenot is still in production, manufactured in the UK by Analog Systems.

▼ **Hammond organ**
Introduced in 1935, the Hammond was the first electric keyboard to establish itself with the public.

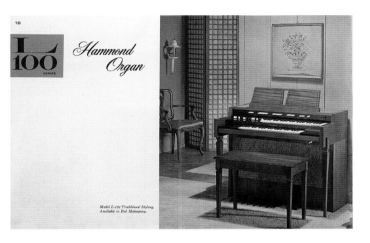

1930s

Many weird and wonderful devices followed. Based in part upon Theremin technology, the Rhythmicon (USA, 1930) was a relatively small instrument with just 17 keys. However, rather than produce continuous notes, it broke these up into rhythms that continued for as long as a key was depressed. Although the technology and the results were primitive, this made it the first "rhythm machine."

More significant, perhaps, was the Trautonium (Germany, 1930), named after its inventor, Friedrich Trautwein. This used a wire pressed against a metal rail to control the pitch of an oscillator; the resistance in the circuit (determined by the position of contact) determined the pitch of the note produced. Additional controls allowed the player to alter the timbre by amplifying or suppressing harmonics, thus making the instrument more flexible than others of the era. The Trautonium was manufactured for domestic use by Telefunken, and several composers wrote works for it. Of these, the most significant was Oskar Sala, who later developed versions of the instrument called the Mixtur-Trautonium and the Concert Trautonium.

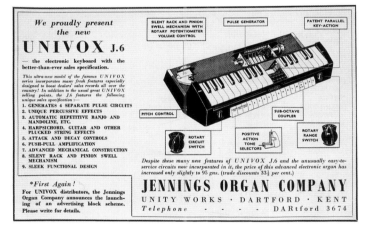

▲ **Univox**
A British magazine advertisement for the Jennings Univox.

Nevertheless, all of these early experiments were overshadowed by the introduction of the Hammond organ (USA, 1935). Based in part upon the tonewheel technology developed for the Telharmonium, this was the first electric keyboard to enter the lives of the public at large. From tiny chapels to the living rooms of the wealthy, the Hammond showed that players and listeners were ready to adopt electrically powered musical instruments, and it was a huge success, musically and commercially. The Hammond can be seen on the DVD that accompanies this book.

Another significant advance was embodied in the Singing Keyboard (USA, 1936). In many ways the forefather of modern samplers, this replayed optical recordings of waveforms (much like early cinema soundtracks) when the player pressed its keys. The same optical technique was used to moderate effect in the early 1960s by Daphne Oram on her Oramics instrument, but perhaps the true descendent of the Singing Keyboard was the Mellotron, which used magnetic tape rather than film, but in many other ways embodied the same concept.

the electronic keyboard story

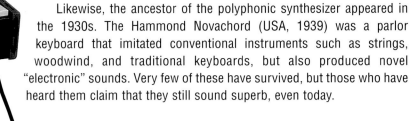

Likewise, the ancestor of the polyphonic synthesizer appeared in the 1930s. The Hammond Novachord (USA, 1939) was a parlor keyboard that imitated conventional instruments such as strings, woodwind, and traditional keyboards, but also produced novel "electronic" sounds. Very few of these have survived, but those who have heard them claim that they still sound superb, even today.

1940s

A number of significant keyboards appeared in the 1940s. The Hammond Solovox (USA, 1940) offered low-pass filters, high-pass filters, primitive envelopes, vibrato, and a knee lever that allowed the performer to control the volume of the sound in real time. It came complete with a dedicated amplifier and speaker in a convenient case that clipped together for easy transportation. If this sounds familiar, it should. This was the precursor to the much more widely known Clavioline (France, 1947) and Jennings Univox (UK, 1951). Used as simple, preset synthesizers, these and similar instruments became mainstays of the 1960s palette of novelty sounds: witness The Beatles' use in "Baby You're a Rich Man," Del Shannon's "Runaway," and, of course, "Telstar" by The Tornados.

The first electric instrument that successfully imitated a range of existing orchestral instruments was almost certainly the Jenny Ondioline invented by Georges Jenny (France, 1941). A rival to Martenot's instrument, the Ondioline was capable of incredible classical, jazz, and traditional solo string (or stringlike) performances.

However, despite their strengths, all of these instruments were monophonic, and articulation remained in the hands of the performer rather than being an aspect of the sound generator itself. To progress further, electronic instruments needed an electrical method to shape the sounds that they produced. That method was "voltage control," which was developed in Canada by Hugh Le Caine, one of the unsung pioneers of music synthesis.

Le Caine had made important contributions in World War II in the fields of radar and nuclear physics and, after the war, he drew upon his knowledge of radio frequency oscillators, frequency modulators, amplitude modulators, and filters to embark upon a project that he called the Electronic Sackbut (Canada, 1945). Possibly the first instrument to use dynamic voltages to shape aspects of the sound, it provided control over timbre and modulation using vertical, lateral, and front-to-back pressure-sensitivity on its keyboard. Later on, Le Caine added a pressure-sensitive left-hand control that, together with the keyboard, allowed the player to modify the waveshape, pitch, amplitude, and modulation of the sound.

The Electronic Sackbut was years ahead of its time, but some of Le Caine's ideas reappeared shortly afterward in the Melochord (Germany 1947). Built by Harald Bode, who would later achieve fame as the inventor of the Bode Frequency Shifter, this allowed the player to trigger envelope shapers and (on a later version) to control the timbre by playing the keys of a second, controller keyboard. Despite its obscurity today, the Melochord was used throughout the

▲ **American Clavioline**
This Clavioline keyboard and amplifier were manufactured in the U.S. by the Chicago Musical Instrument Company, parent to guitar-maker Gibson.

▲ **Clavioline**
Early promotional material for the Clavioline, included in a catalog for British distributor Selmer.

keyboard facts

1950s by leading European avant-garde composers including György Ligeti and Karlheinz Stockhausen.

1950s

By now, technology was advancing at an ever-increasing rate, and two engineers (Harry Olsen and Hebert Belar) seized upon the ideas in a publication called *A Mathematical Theory of Music* to develop a machine that could generate new tunes based upon the analysis of existing songs. The result was the RCA Synthesizer (USA, 1952), which used punched paper as storage, 12 oscillators as sound generators, and basic filters, envelopes, and modulators to shape notes. Inevitably, this did not fulfill its inventors' expectations, but they persevered and developed the RCA Synthesizer MkII. This attracted the attention of the Rockefeller Foundation, which provided the funds for Columbia University to rent the instrument and establish the Columbia-Princeton Electronic Music Center in New York. The Center later attracted some of the leading US-based avant-garde composers, and the era of electronic music had truly arrived.

Elsewhere, the Canadian National Research Council had provided funds for Le Caine to establish an electronic music laboratory in Ottawa, and it was here that he developed the Touch Sensitive Organ (Canada, 1954). This 99-key, fully polyphonic, pressure-sensitive synthesizer/organ was more advanced than anything else at the time and, although Baldwin showed interest in commercializing it, they failed to do so.

At the other end of the scale, the Wurlitzer EP112 electric piano (USA, 1954) was a small, affordable instrument with a high-quality keyboard action that struck reeds rather than strings. For nearly a decade, this was the only electric piano available, and it was therefore a great success. This would later evolve into the EP200, which is still recognized as one of the classic electro-mechanical keyboards. The Wurlitzer can be seen on the DVD that accompanies this book.

▲ **Jenny Ondioline**
Jean-Jacques Perrey, French pioneer of electronic pop, with his Jenny Ondioline in the mid 60s.

Temporarily rivaling electronic keyboards as a means of generating experimental music, *musique concrète* was created by manipulating recordings on strips of magnetic tape. "Dripsody" (which was based on a recording of a single drip of water) was one of the seminal pieces in this genre, and the instrument on which it was created was Le Caine's Special Purpose Tape Recorder (Canada, 1954). This used a keyboard to control the playback of multiple reels of tape and, although the idea wasn't new (others had experimented with changes in pitch and timbre by varying the playback speed of recorded discs) the invention of tape made it possible for Le Caine to extend the principle much further than before. Indeed, there was no reason why the recordings had to be conventional; they could be reversed, layered, filtered, re-recorded, and more. This was sensational stuff, and many avant-garde composers traveled to Canada to make use of the Recorder.

Meanwhile, in the U.S., an inventor named Harry Chamberlin was also experimenting with a tape-replay keyboard. He developed a system that used tapes mounted in such a way that, when you pressed a key, the sound recorded on the tape underneath it was replayed. Chamberlin's system was more practical than Le Caine's: whereas the latter took a single recording and changed its speed to obtain the desired pitches, Chamberlin's instrument—the Chamberlin M1 (USA, 1955)—used individual strips for each note. Unfortunately, the M1 proved to be horribly unreliable, and it was not widely adopted. Nevertheless, as the ancestor of the Mellotron, its place in history is assured.

the electronic keyboard story

1960s

Ahh, the Mellotron. This was the keyboard so famously described as "sounding like dead men singing." What the Hammond organ was to jazz and blues, and the guitar was to rock 'n' roll, the Mellotron was to the "art rock" of the 1960s and "progressive rock" of the 1970s. Indeed, it's probable that neither of the genres could have existed without this keyboard which, nearly half a century after its introduction, is still in production in the UK and Sweden.

The 1960s also saw an explosion in the number of piano-like instruments available. First to arrive was the Hohner Pianet (Germany, 1962), which used metal reeds to create a sound somewhere between that of a musical box and a Wurlitzer electric piano. Successful though the Pianet was, the Clavinet (Germany 1964) was the keyboard that would cement Hohner's place in this history. Simple but remarkably flexible, this could sound like a guitar, a honky-tonk piano, or the embodiment of "funk," simply depending upon how one played it.

Both the Pianet and Clavinet were to remain in production until the 1980s, but the most revered and widely used of all the electric pianos was the Fender Rhodes (USA, 1965). This should have been on sale nearly a decade before but, inexplicably, Leo Fender decided not to release it until 1965. Despite its late entry into the market, and despite the desirability of the existing Wurlitzers and Hohners, the Fender Rhodes became one of the two most widely used electric keyboards in professional music (the other being the Hammond organ) and, after a 25-year hiatus, is again in production in 2008.

Moog System 3P ▲
The "suitcase" version of Moog's modular synthesizer.

The mid-60s also saw the emergence of the first commercial synthesizers. Called "modular" synths (because you could buy discrete modules such as oscillators, filters, and amplifiers, and assemble them according to your specific needs) these were large and unwieldy beasts, and not always reliable, especially in the area of tuning stability. Of these, the most significant (to the extent that all others are almost irrelevant) were those designed and built by Bob Moog in the U.S. Moog was committed to Le Caine's and Bode's concepts of using varying voltages to control aspects of the sound, and he combined these with his own ideas to develop a range of modules that he assembled into remarkable instruments such as the System 3C (1967).

By the late 60s, the synthesizer had finally "arrived," but few bands could afford a Moog, nor did they have the facilities to move the larger ones around or maintain them. There was a huge need for a small, self-contained synthesizer and, in 1969, this was satisfied by a quirky British company, EMS, with its VCS3 (UK, 1969). Nicknamed "The Putney" because of the area of London in which it was built, this proved to be unsuitable for melodic work, but ideal for the generation of sound effects, and it became the mainstay of synthesis in the genres of psychedelia and "space rock."

ARP Sequencer ▲
This ARP model from the late 70s could store one 16-note sequence.

1970s

The 70s were a golden era for keyboard development, and the defining moment was the release of the Minimoog (USA, 1970). Suddenly, a small, transportable instrument could be thrown into the back of a car and be expected to work correctly when it arrived at its destination. What's more, it sounded superb. This changed everything. In 1969, the number of tracks featuring synthesizers could be numbered on your fingers; by the end of the next decade, synthesizers stood shoulder-to-shoulder with guitars as the primary method of music creation. For a few years, all synthesizers were called "Moogs," whether they were built by Moog Music or any of the dozens of other manufacturers that suddenly appeared around the world. Such was the impact of the Minimoog. It can be seen and heard on the DVD that accompanies this book.

If the Minimoog had a limitation, it was that it was monophonic. Competitors such as the ARP 2600 (USA, 1970) and ARP Odyssey (USA, 1972) were duophonic (they could play two notes simultaneously) but keyboard players craved a synthesizer with true polyphony. Unlikely though this now seems, it was the Eminent organ company that gave the world its first new, polyphonic sound: that of the string synthesizer. Using the emerging technology of analog delay lines, the Eminent 310 Unique (Holland, 1972) produced a cornucopia of lush, polyphonic ensemble sounds that would later appear in more limited form on the Eminent Solina (Holland, 1973) and more than 100 other string synths and multi-keyboards.

Other companies were working toward a keyboard instrument that was both polyphonic and capable of the types of sounds created by the Minimoog. First to the market was the Oberheim 4-Voice (USA, 1974), which was essentially a keyboard with four monophonic synthesizers and a voice allocation unit in a single case. But the first true polysynth was much larger, heavier, and more expensive: it was the Yamaha GX-1 (Japan, 1975). This three-manual monster weighed a third of a ton, yet surviving models are generally regarded as the most desirable synthesizers in existence. The reason for this is partly due to their rarity (only seven are known definitely still to exist) but mostly it's because nothing sounds quite as good.

Minimoog
Introduced in 1970, the Minimoog was robust, reliable, and sounded great.

Three years later, Sequential Circuits announced the first polysynth that was light, transportable, and which stored in its memory every parameter that defined its sounds. The Prophet 5 (USA, 1978) was still not cheap, but it quickly became the standard by which all subsequent analog polysynths would be judged.

The Prophet used digital technology to store its analog sounds but, elsewhere, a handful of companies were developing genuine digital synthesizers. In 1978 or thereabouts, New England Digital released the first version of the world's first FM synthesizer, the Synclavier (USA) but the most significant of this new generation of instruments was the Fairlight CMI (Australia, 1979), a combination of additive synthesis, sampling, and primitive multi-track sequencing. Like the Minimoog, the GX-1, and the Prophet before it, this forever changed the way that players thought about making music, and was in large part responsible for the creation of yet another genre of popular music ("electro-pop").

1980s

The next 10 years were to see many technologies become cheaper, smaller, and more widely available. For example, the sampling technology in the Fairlight was to reappear for a fraction of the price in the E-MU Systems Emulator (1981) and then a fraction of that price in instruments such as the Ensoniq Mirage (1986). But more importantly, this was the decade in which all other aspects of music went digital.

the electronic keyboard story

One of the earliest digital synthesizers was the PPG Wave Computer (Germany, 1980), which introduced the idea of a wavetable, snippets of waveforms that could be selected manually or under computer control to create new sounds. Another was the amazingly affordable Casio CT-202 (Japan, 1982), which made some of these delicate "glassy" sounds available to a much wider audience. But by far the most important was the Yamaha DX7 (Japan, 1983), a digital synthesizer that used Frequency Modulation (FM) to generate a huge palette of imitative and previously unheard sounds. Such was the impact of the DX7 that players were soon dumping their Hammonds, Minimoogs, and string synths for next-to-nothing, and you could buy them on the secondhand market for prices that today appear to be insane.

Elsewhere, companies were working on alternative methods of digital synthesis and, in 1986, Roland unveiled Structured Adaptive Synthesis, an early version of "physical modeling," the technique of breaking a sound down mathematically into its component parts and then using a computer to reassemble them when the keyboard is played. SAS was developed to generate piano and piano-type sounds, and it became the basis for a hugely successful range of Roland Digital Pianos such as the RD-1000 (Japan, 1986) and a wide range of domestic models.

▲ Korg M1 and M1R
Korg's M1 keyboard (introduced in 1988) became the most successful "pro" keyboard ever made. The M1R is the rack-mounted version of the M1 workstation.

A far less successful project was the PPG Realiser (Germany, 1986). This was designed to imitate—in digital form—the sound-generating architecture of synthesizers as diverse as the Minimoog and the DX7. Unfortunately, PPG had bitten off more than it could chew, and the company collapsed in 1987, the year in which the Roland D50 (Japan, 1987) appeared. This used a combination of short samples and digitally generated waveforms to create its sounds but, more importantly, was the first synthesizer to contain a high-quality digital effects processor. As a result, the D50 sounded polished in a way that no previous instrument had and, after four years, the curtain came down on the era of the DX7.

Just a year later, Korg swept away even the D50, laying down the template for the modern keyboard workstation. The Korg M1 (Japan, 1988) combined high-quality, sample-based synthesis, the ability to layer up to eight sounds or distribute them across the keyboard, two digital effects units, and a radically new multi-timbral architecture. It became the most successful "pro" keyboard ever released, and every modern keyboard workstation—whether designed for professional or domestic use—owes much of its fundamental structure to the M1.

1990 to the present day

Although the Realiser had flopped, some of its concepts were sound, and other companies had the resources to develop a true "physical modeling" instrument. First to the market was the Yamaha VL1 (Japan, 1994). This duophonic synthesizer emulated a number of existing orchestral instruments, but was also capable of a huge range of novel sounds, some reminiscent of real-world instruments, others unique to the synth.

Strangely, Yamaha failed to recognize where the greatest opportunity for its

keyboard facts

new technology lay, and failed to capitalize on its leadership in the field. A much smaller company, Clavia, realized that modeling could be used to recreate and extend the architecture and sounds of analog synthesis, and its Nord Lead (Sweden, 1995) became the world's first "virtual analog" synthesizer.

A few weeks later, Korg announced two modeling synths: the monophonic Prophecy (Japan, 1995), and the polyphonic, multi-timbral OASYS. Of these, the latter was never to appear in commercial form, but the former was a significant success. Offering a range of models including orchestral instruments, electro-mechanical instruments, and numerous forms of analog synthesis, it remains a very flexible soloing instrument.

A version of the Prophecy was also designed as an upgrade board for the Korg Trinity (Japan, 1995). For seven years, the structure introduced on the M1 had remained largely unchanged, and it had been adopted by all the other workstation manufacturers. The Trinity was the next step forward: a workstation that allowed the player to select and allocate up to 10 internal effects units in a truly multi-timbral architecture.

Of course, the hearts of the Trinity and its ilk were microprocessors dressed up in keyboards and dedicated control panels, so it was inevitable that the music industry and the computer industry would begin to move closer together, to the point where it might become difficult to distinguish one from the other. This was exemplified by the Clavia Nord Modular (Sweden, 1997), which combined a dedicated processor unit with programming and control software running on a Macintosh or PC. Another approach was pioneered by Digidesign, who had supplied a pair of "soft" modular synthesizers—Softsynth (USA, 1986) and Turbosynth (USA, 1988)—that ran on Macintosh computers alongside its Sound Tools recording and editing system. These paved the way for the emergence of the modern breed of softsynths which—more often than not—seek to imitate a specific vintage synthesizer. This in turn paved the way for yet another marriage of PC and music keyboard, embodied in the Open Labs Neko 64 (USA, 2004) and the Muse Research Receptor (USA, 2005), which were PC motherboards dressed up with keyboards and dedicated control panels.

The Korg OASYS (Japan, 2005), which had little in common with the original OASYS announced 10 years earlier, was a better solution. This enclosed a PC motherboard, but its operating system, based on Linux, was written specifically for the instrument, thus making it far more robust and reliable than keyboards that seemed ostensibly similar, but which ran standard PC applications on top of Microsoft Windows. At the time of writing there are seven synthesizers—sample-based, physical modeling, FM, and virtual analog—residing within the OASYS, and these have been seamlessly married to many of the ground-breaking technologies of the past two decades: vector synthesis, wave sequencing, KARMA, MIDI sequencing and hard-disk recording.

Together with Roland's VariPhrase sound manipulation technology, introduced in 2000 and most recently updated in the V-Synth GT (Japan, 2006), the OASYS represents the current pinnacle of commercial electronic keyboard technology. A century after the Choralcelo and Telharmonium, these instruments would have been unimaginable to Melvin Severy and Thaddeus Cahill. Who can say what the next 100 years will bring?

▲ Korg OASYS
Seven synthesizers reside within the case of the Korg OASYS, as well as a MIDI sequencer and hard-disk recorder.

the electronic keyboard story

3
the
instruments

Keyboard Profiles

By Gordon Reid

The Hammond organ (1935)

Long before there was rock 'n' roll, there was the ancestor of the first and greatest of the rock 'n' roll keyboards. Designed in the 1930s, this was the Hammond "tonewheel" organ, so-called because the electrical signals that were the basis of its sound were generated by noncircular discs (tonewheels) rotating in a magnetic field.

Tonewheels had been introduced on Thaddeus Cahill's monstrous Telharmonium in 1906, but Laurens Hammond (who was a prolific innovator and a first-class engineer) realized that they could form the basis of an affordable and transportable instrument if he could reduce the sound generator to a manageable size. This he did, at the same time marrying it to a system of "drawbars" that allowed players to control the loudness of the harmonics that contributed to each note. This was a stroke of genius; just nine drawbars contributed to each voice, and each had just nine volume levels, but this offered hundreds of millions of possible registrations!

In truth, Hammond had developed the instrument as a vehicle for a synchronous motor that he had invented for his clocks, and it was therefore the Hammond Clock Company that unveiled the Model A organ in April 1935. Envisaged as a substitute for a pipe organ, this received almost universal acclaim and went into production in June. The following year, the Model BC added a second bank of detuned tonewheels, which gave the instrument a richer, chorused sound and almost certainly made it the first "ensemble" keyboard. Then, as the decade progressed, the company introduced the Models C, D, and Concert Model E, and the Aeolian player-organ, which was the equivalent of a player-piano, using paper rolls to replay pre-recorded performances.

In 1937, a chap named Don Leslie bought one of the first Hammonds, expecting it to sound like a pipe organ. Unfortunately, it proved to be a disappointment, and he decided that the missing element was the natural movement that occurs when the sounds of hundreds of pipes interact.

In an attempt to emulate this, he experimented with many configurations of rotating and static speakers, trying different speeds and phase arrangements, connecting and disconnecting speakers until, almost by accident, he found that he obtained a very pleasing effect using a single rotating speaker. The experiments continued: Leslie replaced the rotating speakers with static speakers directed at rotating horn assemblies and, in 1940, after a few further refinements,

Hammond A-100 ▲
This model, introduced in 1959, had built-in reverberation, amplification, and loudspeakers.

he released his dual-speaker rotary system. It seems that Laurens Hammond hated this, and even went as far as to release a "Leslie-proof" organ that wouldn't power up without a Hammond-manufactured speaker connected. Fortunately, the rest of the world had a different view, and the Hammond plus Leslie "combo" was born.

Elsewhere, Hammond continued to innovate, releasing the remarkable Novachord, the forerunner of today's polyphonic synthesizers, and the Solovox, the precursor to the better-known Clavioline. The company was also expanding its range of tonewheel organs, launching spinet models and even models with the sound generators from the Novachord and Solovox built in. Nevertheless, the most important development in the 1940s was that of the "scanner" chorus/vibrato generator.

Until this point, Hammonds had featured two effects: tremolo, and the chorus generated by the second bank of tonewheels. The scanner unit superseded the tremolo, and—in many people's view—made the older, heavier and much more expensive chorus generator obsolete. The stage was set.

In 1955, the company unveiled the

Model B-3 and the almost identical Model C-3, both of which embodied everything that was best about Hammond organs. Then, in 1959, these were joined by the Model A-100, the same instrument but with a built-in reverb unit, amplification and speakers. (This made the A-100 the first self-contained model of the larger "console" tonewheel organs.)

Coupled to one or more Leslie speakers, the B-3 and its siblings could be jazzy or refined, and were as at home in nightclubs as they were in chapels. Indeed, players such as Fats Waller had introduced Hammonds to rhythm & blues and jazz almost as soon as they had appeared in the mid 30s. However, it was in the emerging genres of pop, rock, and soul music that these organs were to achieve their greatest fame. Nothing else in the keyboard world could snarl or scream like a B-3 so, for the first time, the keyboard player could be the focus of attention, not the accompanist.

Mind you, mastering a big Hammond was not trivial. The best players didn't just play the right notes, they articulated the sound using the swell pedal, by selecting presets as the music demanded, by pulling and pushing the drawbars to change the voicing dynamically, and most importantly by flicking the Leslie speed control to add expression. Nonetheless, many became highly skilled, not just mastering the instrument in a technical sense, but also developing individual styles that are admired to this day. From the harder-edged bebop and blues of Jimmy Smith to the gospel of Billy Preston, from the rhythm & blues of Booker T to the gospel-inspired rock of Steve Winwood, all the way to the incredible dexterity of prog-rocker Keith Emerson, a Hammond was not just the instrument of choice; it was the only sensible choice.

Throughout the 1960s, B-3s and C-3s dominated the sound of popular music, providing the soundtrack to the massive cultural changes of the era, and Hammond continued to release new tonewheel models including the popular L-100, the radical X-66, and the enormous G-100. Furthermore, Laurens Hammond and Don Leslie buried the hatchet in 1966 (and not in each other) and the first Hammond to incorporate a Leslie speaker appeared soon after. This was not a classic, but later variations would prove to be more successful. Then there were cut-down instruments such as the T-100 and T-200 which, due to their low cost,

proved to be very popular with all manner of rock and pop bands.

In 1973, Laurens Hammond died and, in 1975, after a short, final manufacturing run of B-3s and C-3s (the A-100 had been discontinued in 1965) the tonewheel generator was discarded. By this time, keyboard players were predominantly interested in synthesizers, and the Hammond organ was beginning to fall from favor. The company continued to develop interesting organs, but these failed to recapture the magic of the previous decade and when, in the 1980s, it embraced the new technologies of digital voicing and MIDI, the time of the electro-mechanical organ seemed past.

Happily, this era did not last long and, in the mid 90s, a new generation of musicians discovered the B-3 and its brethren, finding that there was no substitute for the "real thing." Nowadays, Hammond is owned by Suzuki, and produces a range of digital organs that seek primarily to emulate the B-3 and C-3. There is a simple reason for this; nothing has ever sounded better. Coupled to a large Leslie speaker, these organs were responsible for much of the jazz, blues, soul, and rock music of the past 70 years, and—despite the fact that the youngest of these classics is already more than 30 years old—it seems that they will continue to do so for the foreseeable future. The Hammond can be seen on the DVD with this book.

The Mellotron (1963)

Back in the 1950s, a Californian window cleaner named Bill Fransen was intrigued by the sounds emanating from one of his customers' garages and, peering through a (newly cleaned?) window, he espied a remarkable contraption. Named after its inventor, Harry Chamberlin, the Chamberlin MusicMaster pioneered the use of pre-recorded tapes mounted inside a keyboard instrument in such a way that, whenever you pressed a key, the sound recorded on the tape below it emerged from the instrument's speakers. Fransen introduced himself and ended up working as Chamberlin's salesman. Unfortunately, the MusicMaster proved to be very temperamental, not least because its electronics were badly supported, the tape guides could go awry, and because it hummed badly.

Two years later, a company based

in Birmingham, England, was intrigued to receive an order from Fransen for 70 matched tape heads. Curious as to why anyone should require so many matched heads, they met and eventually joined forces with Fransen who, unbeknown to Chamberlin, had come to the UK to find the skills and finance to build and sell the instruments. Fortunately, the Bradley family (hence the company name, Bradmatic) not only had the skills to build Chamberlins, but also to refine them. However, like Fransen, they didn't have the money, so they advertised for support. Bandleader and radio broadcaster Eric Robinson replied, and development of an improved instrument began.

The marriage of Fransen, Bradmatic, and Robinson was made in heaven: Fransen proved to be a talented recording engineer, and the Eric Robinson Organisation owned the highly regarded IBC Studios which were to be used to record the tapes that would eventually be installed within the new keyboard. Shortly thereafter, the Eric Robinson Organisation was renamed Mellotronics Ltd., and its first product, the Mellotron Mark 1 (the name of which was derived from MELLifluOus elecTRONics) appeared in 1963. Costing £1,000 (equivalent to $2,800 then), a huge sum at that time, these Mellotrons offered many improvements over Chamberlin's instruments, but remained rather unreliable, and it was to be another year before the first truly playable Mellotron was to appear.

The Mark 2 Mellotron was a 350-lb. dual-manual monster containing more than 70 ⅜-inch tape players, a reverb unit, amplifiers, and speakers. It was 70-note polyphonic and was able to reproduce all manner of sounds including orchestral strings, flutes, brass, guitars, organs, pianos and choirs, the last of which were famously described as sounding "like dead men singing." A second and even more expensive version, the Mark 2 FX Console, was designed for use as a sound effects machine in TV and film studios.

Unfortunately, Mellotronics still saw the Mellotron as a type of organ and sold several instruments to clubs and theaters, while others became the parlor novelties of glitterati such as Peter Sellers, who later gave his Mark 2 to Princess Margaret! Despite this, the pop and rock community took the Mellotron to its heart, and it was this that ensured its success. By 1967, everyone was experimenting with it, and The Beatles had already recorded what was eventually to become the most famous Mellotron performance of all time; the introduction to "Strawberry Fields Forever." But the band that deserves the most credit for bringing the instrument to the world's attention was The Moody Blues. Their 1967 hit "Nights In White Satin" was probably the first track to bridge the gulf between "beat" music and classical orchestration.

In 1968, a smaller and cheaper Mellotron appeared. Called the Model 300, this dispensed with one of the keyboards and the internal speakers, and adopted a new tape format with redesigned motors and electronics. Unfortunately, its mechanism had an Achilles heel, and its tapes were prone to wrapping themselves around the large drums that formed part of the sound selection mechanism. Nevertheless, bands such as Barclay James Harvest and Gentle Giant were influential exponents of the Model 300.

Two years later, the Mark 2 and Model 300 made way for a much cheaper instrument: the Model 400, which was launched with a price tag of just £795 (equivalent to $1,900 then). This weighed barely a third as much as a Mark 2, making it much more transportable than any previous Mellotron, and this stimulated an explosion in the number of keyboard players using the instrument. The customer list quickly became a "who's who" of the industry, but it was in the genre of progressive rock that the Mellotron became best known, and the huge popularity of bands such as Genesis and Yes was due in no small part to their sounds.

In 1975 the final Mellotron appeared, the Mark V, which was essentially two Model 400s in a single case. But in 1976, the bubble burst. The advent of cheap string machines and polyphonic synthesizers made it much simpler for keyboard players to obtain orchestral textures, and the birth of punk rock meant that they no longer wanted to.

Overnight, the Mellotron became a dinosaur and when, in 1977, Mellotronics' U.S. distributor collapsed while owing it a large sum of money, the company was unable to meet its financial obligations and was liquidated.

Happily, Streetly Electronics—the former Bradmatic—survived, and continued manufacturing instruments. However, they couldn't call them Mellotrons because the receiver had

sold the name along with the physical assets of Mellotronics Ltd. Without the rights to the name, another was needed, and thus the Novatron was born.

There were four Novatrons: the Model 400SM, the 400FX, the Mark V, and the T.550. Of these, only the T.550 was a new product, the others being re-badged Mellotrons. (Manuals of the era reminded readers that, "we are no longer able to use the name Mellotron" and asked them to "substitute the new name Novatron in its place when reading this manual.")

Punk rock and its new-wave offshoot lasted for four years or so but, in the early 80s, there was a resurgence of interest in progressive rock, with bands such as Pallas championing the

Mellotron 400 ▲
Cheaper and more transportable

Mellotron once again. Unfortunately, the advent of cheap digital samplers meant that, for most players, the Mellotron was obsolete so, in 1986, Streetly Electronics went into voluntary liquidation, and the Mellotron died.

Except that it didn't. Interest in Mellotrons never waned, and numerous companies experimented with tape replay instruments based upon it. In 1991, an American named Dave Kean purchased the rights to the Mellotron name and established Mellotron Archives. In the UK, Martin Smith and John Bradley (the son of one of the Mellotron's original designers, Les Bradley) reformed Streetly Electronics. Both companies supplied tapes and spare parts, but by the middle of the 1990s the demand for refurbished Mellotrons was reaching the point where there were not enough vintage instruments to satisfy demand. It was therefore inevitable that somebody would look again at manufacturing Mellotrons.

In 2002, Kean and his Swedish

collaborator, Marcus Resch, started shipping the Mellotron Mark VI, a clone of the Model 400. Then, in 2006, Smith and Bradley launched the Model 4000, which combines a modified version of the tape replay mechanism from a Mark 2 in a case approximately the size (and convenience) of a Model 400. Amazingly, after 44 years, the best Mellotrons ever built are those being built today!

The Hohner Clavinet (1963)

In the early 1950s, professional keyboard players were, essentially, organists. Then, in 1954, the first of the Wurlitzer electric pianos appeared. Strangely, this did not lead to a flood of competitors, and the next electric keyboard to reach the public was not another piano, but a form of harpsichord. Invented by Ernst Zacharias and manufactured by Hohner in Germany, it was called the Cembalet, and it appeared in 1958.

Like a harpsichord, the Cembalet plucked something to create a sound, but unlike a harpsichord, that something was a flat metal reed rather than a string. The vibration in the reed was then detected by a pickup, amplified, and directed to a speaker. This mechanism was later modified in another instrument developed by Zacharias, the Hohner Pianet, which was apparently based on a patent dating all the way back to the 1920s, but which first appeared in 1962. In the Pianet, each key was mounted on a pivoting metal bar, onto the back of which a slightly sticky pad was slid. The pad sat on top of, and in contact with, the reed, pressing it down so that it was under a bending strain. When the player depressed the key, the pad lifted, not just allowing the reed to spring straight but also pulling it upward for a fraction of an inch before the adhesion was broken.

The Pianet "L," "C," and "N" were the first three keyboards to bear the name, and these were soon followed by the Combo Pianet, which was the gigging version, with no lid or internal amplification. All of these models used essentially the same mechanism, with leather pads, electrostatic pickups, and active electronics. Because of their bright sound, these are now viewed as the "classic" Pianets.

Two years after launching the Pianet, Hohner unveiled another Zacharias invention. Modeled on the clavichord and developed from a prototype called the Claviphon, this used strings rather than reeds and, rather than being plucked, these were hit by rubber hammers. There was no sustain: notes could ring out while the keys were held down, but were immediately damped upon release, Nevertheless the mechanism was velocity-sensitive, and it generated a very different tone depending upon whether you played notes aggressively or gently. It was also pressure-sensitive, and if you leaned on a key, you could sharpen the pitch slightly for guitarlike vibrato effects. This instrument had a unique sound—like a guitar at the top end, and deeply metallic at the bottom—and it went on sale in 1964. It was the Hohner Clavinet.

The first model was called the Clavinet 1. Designed for home use and classical music, it was surprisingly heavy, and came complete with spindly wooden legs. Electrically, it offered just two rocker switches for changing the tone, a volume control, and included a small in-built, battery-powered amplifier and speaker. The Clavinet 2—which omitted the amplifier and speaker—followed soon after. In all likelihood, this was aimed at the bands of the era, but it was not a great hit.

This all changed when Hohner unveiled the distinctive, white and red Clavinet "C" in 1968. Although this retained much of the electronics of the "1" and "2," including the dual-switch arrangement, it featured modified pickups that generated a slightly different sound than before and, sometime during its life, it gained the damper bar that was later to define much of the Clavinet sound.

A slider to the right of the keyboard moved the bar such that, at one extreme, it allowed the strings to vibrate freely, but at the other extreme it muted them so that each note was no more than a pitched "thunk." This increased the flexibility of the Clavinet considerably, and the "C" is now considered by some aficionados to be the most desirable of all Clavinets. Indeed, this was the instrument used by Stevie Wonder on "Superstition," which is often quoted to be the archetypal Clavinet track.

The "C" was the only Clavinet to be built elsewhere under licence: a version called the Echolette Beat Spinet had reversed keys and sported a different color scheme, but it was in every other way a Clavinet "C." Another oddity that appeared alongside the "C" was the

Clavinet "L," a bizarre version with no tone or volume controls, no damper, but reversed colored keys, and three (!) legs. This was not a great success and is the rarest of all Clavinets.

In 1971, Hohner updated the instrument again, and in doing so created a classic. Powered by a 9V battery, or an optional power adapter, it had no amp or speaker, but improved electronics that offered six rocker switches: two that selected combinations of its two pickups, and four that selected filters—Brilliant, Treble, Medium, and Soft—that you could use in any combination to create a huge range of timbres. With its amazingly funky sound, it was adopted by the likes of Billy Preston, Herbie Hancock and The Commodores, but also found itself used in every other genre of 1970s music, from the pop of Status Quo and Abba to the progressive rock of Emerson Lake & Palmer, to Supertramp to Led Zeppelin . . . and almost everybody else.

Late in its life, the D6 appeared in a very different guise, housed in a much more roadworthy case covered in black vinyl, with heavy, rubbery end-cheeks. Then, in 1977, this metamorphosed into the Clavinet E7, which looked almost identical to the revised D6, but with small differences in the control layout. Internally, it was also very similar, but it featured better shielding and a filter that made it less susceptible to buzzes and hums caused by electrical interference.

Elsewhere, Hohner had also updated the Pianets, replacing all the earlier models with the Pianet "M" (domestic) and "T" (stage) models. These were very different from their predecessors; the reeds were less bright, the leather pads were replaced by silicone rubber, and the electrostatic pickups had been replaced by electromagnetic ones. Cosmetically, the "T" was clearly the sibling of the E7 and in 1978 the two were combined to create the last instrument in the family, the Duo, which allowed players to select various combinations of the Pianet and Clavinet, layering the sounds or playing them independently either side of a keyboard split. Some players felt that the Clavinet sound was harmed in the Duo, but the argument was moot because it was released just as affordable polysynths were starting to appear, and the whole Clavinet and Pianet family fell out of favor in the early 1980s.

For a decade or more, there was little interest in Clavinets, but a

significant resurgence has occurred in recent years, and a number of companies service them and supply spare parts such as hammers, strings and pickups. This is just as well: the pads of a heavily pounded Clavinet will eventually split and grab the string as you play it, degrading the sound and causing a nasty thump when keys are released. But an instrument in good condition remains a joy to play (especially through an array of effects pedals) and, even today, there's nothing that sounds quite as funky as a Clavinet. The Clavinet can be seen on the DVD that accompanies this book.

The Fender Rhodes (1965)

Born in 1910, Harold Rhodes was just 20 when he found himself running a chain of piano schools across the U.S. A little over a decade later, he was asked to provide music therapy for wounded soldiers, and designed a 2.5-octave piano using hammers and cut-down aluminium pipes from B-17 bombers as the sound sources. Called the Army Air Corps Piano, or sometimes the Xylette, it was small enough to be transported easily and proved to be a huge success, with around 125,000 manufactured during the latter stages of World War II.

Following the war, Rhodes established the Rhodes Piano Corporation and, in 1946, launched a 3.5-octave electro-mechanical piano named the "Pre-Piano" or the "Bantam." This retained much of the Xylette design, but proved to be unreliable so, in 1949, he invented a piano that used hammers and a form of tuning fork comprising a cylindrical "tine" and a resonator as its sound source. He built a 72-note instrument and demonstrated this widely, attracting the attention of Leo Fender, who was so impressed that he bought into the company. Unfortunately, Fender was not impressed enough to build the full-range pianos that Rhodes was developing so, from 1959 to 1964, the 32-note Piano Bass was the only Fender Rhodes manufactured.

In retrospect, this was a strange decision. A contemporary of Rhodes, Ben Meissner, had also invented a stringless piano in the 1930s. This had an action not dissimilar to a grand piano, but used vibrating steel reeds as sound sources. With electrostatic pickups, an amplifier and built-in speakers, this had a beautiful tone.

Meissner's ideas were adopted in the 1950s by Wurlitzer, a company already well-known for its organs and jukeboxes, and in 1954 they launched a 64-note instrument called the EP-112. This meant that all early recordings with electric piano featured Wurlitzers and, until the launch of the Hohner Pianet in 1962, Wurlitzer had the market to itself.

In 1963, Fender printed a catalog that showed two electro-mechanical pianos—the Piano 61 and Piano 73—that don't seem to have made it into full production. News of Rhodes' developments then reached CBS who, after visiting his workshop, offered to buy Fender's stake in the company for $13 million, a huge sum in the mid 1960s. Fender agreed and, in 1965, Rhodes began manufacturing the Fender Rhodes Electric Piano, variations of which would remain in production for 16 years. Other models would come and go, but the Electric Piano in its various guises—most notably the "Mark 1" Suitcase 73 and Stage 73, and their younger but larger siblings the Suitcase 88 and Stage 88—soon became standard equipment for almost every serious jazz keyboard player in the world. Early users included Chick Corea, Duke Ellington, Herbie Hancock, and Joe Zawinul, and when Billy Preston played one on The Beatles' *Let It Be*, the instrument's place in history was assured.

The differences between the models were obvious. Firstly, the 73s had 73-note keyboards and the 88s offered full 88-note keyboards. Equally obvious, the Suitcase models came complete with 50W amplifiers and speakers that attached to the piano itself for transportation. This made the instruments completely self-contained but monstrously heavy. The Stage models had no amplifier or speakers, which made them more attractive to bands, and the smallest, lightest, and cheapest of the four—the Stage 73—quickly became the "classic" Fender Rhodes piano.

Throughout the early and mid 70s, Fender Rhodes dominated the market. Mind you, the Wurlitzer was still a significant instrument, and the EP200 (introduced in 1969) was every bit as important to some players as the Fender Rhodes was to others; the sound of Supertramp and The Carpenters (for example) would have been very different without it. But despite being bigger and heavier, despite a heavy action that—if badly set-up—could be very hard to play, and

despite lacking the EP200's tremolo on early models, the Fender Rhodes was never challenged as the number one instrument in its class. The reason for this was simple: neither piano, bell nor glockenspiel, but a bit of each, it sounded great and was incredibly flexible. Indeed, the sound could differ significantly depending upon the hammer tips used as well as the positions and angles of the pickups. With a good amplifier and a selection of effects units such as chorus, phasing and wah-wah, it could be almost anything you wanted it to be.

In 1974, the name "Fender" was removed, although there were no physical modifications associated with this other than the change of the nameplates. After this, numerous upgrades followed, including improvements to the hammer tips and tone bars, plus new electronics, amplifiers, and speaker systems. There was even a 3rd-party modification called Dyno-My-Piano, which made the instrument even brighter and more cutting than before.

For a decade, the Stage 73 and EP200 remained almost unchallenged as the electric pianos of choice but, in 1977, Yamaha announced the first of its "CP" series of electric grand pianos. These were to become hugely successful among players who wanted

a more authentic piano sound and, for the first time, interest in the established manufacturers began to wane. Furthermore, the arrival of polyphonic synthesizers capable of piano-like sounds was to eat deeply into Rhodes' market.

In response, Rhodes introduced Mark II versions in 1979, and these are easily recognized by the flat tops that let you place other keyboards on top of them. Then, in 1980, two new models appeared: the Rhodes 54, and the Rhodes Mark III (also called the EK-10), which was a curious hybrid of a Rhodes piano and a primitive synthesizer. Launched in 1982, The last model in the CBS era was a domestic version of the Suitcase 88.

In 1983, William Schultz, the head of CBS, bought Rhodes and, in 1984, the new company released its only product, the Rhodes Stage 73 Mark V, of which three prototypes were even equipped with MIDI. But this was the year after the DX7 appeared, and its electric piano patch had already swept aside all the genuine electro-mechanical pianos. Thereafter, the Rhodes brand was stagnant and, in 1987, Roland bought the company, eventually producing the Rhodes MK-60, MK-80, Model 660, Model 760, and VK-1000, all of which were digital instruments. Good though these

▲ **Fender Rhodes**
This model is the Suitcase 88.

proved to be, Harold Rhodes did not like digital technology and, after an abortive attempt to interest the Japanese in manufacturing a genuine electro-mechanical piano, he entered negotiations with them to buy back his name. He eventually did so in 1997, and founded the Rhodes Music Corporation, declaring that he would design and launch the best electric piano yet. Unfortunately, time ran out. No new instruments appeared, and Rhodes himself died from pneumonia in December 2000.

In 2007, the Rhodes Music Corporation—run by Rhodes' former colleague Joseph Brandstetter—announced the impending release of Harold Rhodes' dream: three new models, all called the Mark 7, each to be made available in 61-, 73-, and 88-note versions. Promising an improved action, improved electronics, and many modern features such as an advanced MIDI specification, it remains to be seen whether these will, indeed, be the best electric pianos ever. The Rhodes can be seen on the DVD with this book.

The Minimoog (1970)

Here's an easy one: What do ballpoint pens and synthesizers have in common? Answer: they have both, at one time or another, been named after their inventors; the Biro brothers and Dr. Robert Moog (which, to set the record straight, rhymes with "vogue"). Even today, a quarter of a century after the original Moog Music bit the corporate dust, there are people for whom all synthesizers are "Moogs." This is doubly impressive, because I lied: Bob Moog didn't invent the synthesizer, he started out building another man's electronic musical instrument: the Theremin. Nevertheless, his work on voltage control in 1963, and the groundbreaking modular synthesizers he designed and built in the mid and late 1960s cemented his place in history, even before the development of the most important monosynth ever released.

During the late 60s, R. A. Moog Inc. employed two engineers named Gene Zumchack and Bill Hemsath, and it was they who first badgered Bob Moog into considering the development of an integrated synthesizer that players could use without resorting to the spaghetti junction of patch leads

necessary for creating sounds on Moog's large, modular synthesizers. Strangely, Moog declined to develop these ideas, and Zumchack left, subsequently designing an integrated synthesizer—the Sonic V—for a company named muSonics (which, in a bizarre twist of fate, was merged with R A Moog in 1970 to create Moog/muSonics, shortly thereafter renamed Moog Music Inc).

Meanwhile, not everything was rosy at R. A. Moog. Bob Moog's engineering credentials may have been of a high order, but his business acumen was not. Despite the explosion of interest in electronic music in the late 1960s (fueled in part by the album *Switched on Bach* by Walter Carlos) his company was insolvent. Fortunately, employees

▲ **Dr. Robert Moog**

Jim Scott, Chad Hunt and Bill Hemsath had continued to hassle him into pursuing Zumchack's ideas. Without the determination of these men, Moog would have gone bankrupt, and his name might have been consigned to relative obscurity alongside other synthesizer pioneers of the mid to late 60s. Fortunately, before the financial situation became terminal, the team developed an integrated synth closely related to the Moog Modular System 10 (which itself had been codeveloped by Zumchack). After building three prototypes, they ignored Moog's explicit instructions not to go into production and, while he was away on a trip, they built the first batch of Minimoogs. Had the decision been left in Bob Moog's hands, it is very likely that the world's most revered monosynth would never have existed.

At the time of its introduction at the AES Convention in October 1970, the Minimoog was a revolution in design, combining many of the features of its behemoth modular forebears within an ergonomically beautiful, eminently playable and surprisingly affordable instrument. At first, music stores didn't see its potential but, within a handful of years, everybody had a Minimoog (or two) sitting on top of their Hammonds, Rhodes pianos, Clavinets, and Mellotrons, and its bass and lead sounds soon became the standards by which all others would be measured.

Different authorities offer different reasons for the appeal of the Minimoog sound, including the inconsistencies of the oscillators, the mild distortion imparted by the filter, and serendipitous errors in the shape of its contour generators. Interestingly, codesigner Jim Scott (who developed those contour generators) has gone on record to say that it should be attributed to a series of accidents. Indeed, when Moog and others later attempted to correct some of these "faults," they found that the perceived sound quality was degraded.

Contrary to myth, all Minimoogs were Model Ds; models A, B, and C were prototypes never offered to the public. Nevertheless, there were variations on the basic theme. Generally unavailable in the UK, options included a pitch ribbon that could be fitted to replace the pitch wheel, a split keyboard/control panel that allowed players to indulge in guitarist-style posing, and multiple triggering. The only area in which the synthesizer itself changed considerably between its introduction and the end of production was in the design of its oscillators. The first 299 units used discrete oscillators, which meant that there were no chips in them, and many players believe that these models sound the best. The next 9,000 or so used a newer design based on a chip called the 3046, while the last 3,000 or thereabouts were based on a more stable chip called the uA726. The sounds of the three versions were subtly different, but in the late 70s and early 80s many owners updated older Minimoogs by replacing the earlier boards with later ones, so a low serial number is no guarantee of what's inside the case.

Three years after the Minimoog appeared, a plethora of alternatives began to appear on the market. More affordable instruments from Japanese companies such as Roland, Korg, and Yamaha, while sounding thinner and

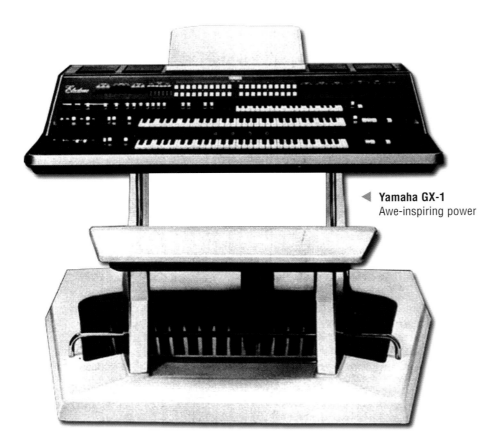

Yamaha GX-1
Awe-inspiring power

less engaging, offered significantly enhanced facilities, and they soon began to make substantial inroads into Moog's sales. Yet, by remaining the Rolls-Royce of the industry, the Minimoog hung on until 1981, by which time micro-processor controlled synthesizers such as the Prophet 5 and the Oberheim OBX offered all the advantages of an excellent sound plus memories and polyphony. So Norlin Music (the company that had bought Moog Music in 1973) stopped producing the Minimoog, replacing it with the Source. This was cheaper, lighter, stable, and it sounded great. But the era of the dedicated monosynth was over. The Source was not a success, and the Moog brand disappeared in 1984.

The Minimoog was the first stage-worthy synthesizer that could do battle with (and win a battle against) a guitarist, and at a stroke it changed the face of modern music. Furthermore, because it gave players access to the building blocks of sound, it allowed them for the first time to create signature sounds for themselves and their bands.

But, despite the enormous influence that it wielded over future synthesizer designs (it wasn't until the launch of the Yamaha DX7 in 1983 that the mould was broken) only 12,242 Minimoogs were built. The last one

(serial number 13259) was presented to Bob Moog at the NAMM show in 1981, four years after he left the company that still bore his name.

Today, the Minimoog is perhaps the single most commonly sought-after piece of synthesizer equipment, and is still considered by many to be the best-sounding monosynth ever created. Consequently, there have been numerous attempts to clone it, most notably by Alex Winter, who obtained the rights to the Moog name in the UK and in 1998 built a handful of updated instruments in Wales. None of these clones were particularly successful but, in 2003, Bob Moog himself wrote the next chapter in the Minimoog's history. He regained the rights to his name, changed the name of his current company from Big Briar to Moog Music Inc, and subsequently released the Minimoog Voyager. But this failed to replace the original Minimoog in the hearts of keyboard players. Even today, the Minimoog remains the king of the lead and bass synthesizers. It can be seen on the DVD with this book.

The Yamaha GX-1 (1975)

Let's embark upon a flight of fancy. It's Christmas 1975 and you're so mind-bogglingly wealthy that you can afford

any toy that takes your fancy. You have Hammonds, a room full of Mellotrons, every electric piano on the planet, plus Minimoogs and ARPs galore. You even own some of those funny little string synths that have just started to appear. Now you're after something a bit special: for instance, something that allows you to play huge chords, rumbling bass, and soaring lead lines concurrently, that can emulate orchestral instruments and other synthesizers with ease, and that has a sound that can simultaneously shatter glass, shake mountains, and wake the dead.

Surprisingly, there's nothing fundamentally wrong with this scenario. In early 1975, keyboard rigs consisted exclusively of organs, Mellotrons, electric pianos, clavinets, "strings" and monosynths. It was onto this stage that Yamaha launched a synthesizer that looked like nothing so much as a huge, white, and extremely heavy organ. Weighing in at 660lbs for the three-manual console, plus 190lbs for the bass pedals and stand, plus a further 620lbs for a pair of its massive 240-watt speaker enclosures, it could do everything suggested above, and it cost $60,000. It was the mighty Yamaha GX-1.

How can one describe the GX-1 in just a couple of pages? In an era before most players had even seen a polysynth, it didn't evoke mere respect; it evoked awe. But to understand this today, you have to read the following description as if you had never seen a synthesizer that could play two sounds simultaneously, or even three notes simultaneously.

The basic building block of a GX-1 sound was called a Tone, and this comprised a multiple-waveform VCO, dual (high-pass and low-pass) resonant filters, a VCA, and dual-contour generators. However, you couldn't sit down at a GX-1 alone and program a Tone; you needed a dedicated programmer that looked like the top panel of an analog monosynth. Once you had programmed your sound on this, you could use another contraption called a Setting Box to transfer it into a matchbox-sized Tone Cartridge that you then inserted into the GX-1 itself. This might seem long-winded, but three years before the advent of the Z80 microprocessor allowed Sequential Circuits to incorporate 40 patch memories into the Prophet 5, the GX-1 offered 70 Tone memories with none of the parameter quantisation of microprocessor-controlled synths.

keyboard facts

The GX-1 had two, eight-voice polyphonic manuals, upper and lower, of which the upper offered touch- (side-to-side) sensitivity. Each of the 16 notes that you could play on these manuals were created by not one, but two of the Tones described above, and these could be programmed to produce completely different sounds if you wished, or similar ones to create ensembles, or even complementary ones that could be mixed to create complex, evolving sounds. The GX-1 also offered a set of bass pedals that, far from producing the simple bass sounds of conventional organs, was the most highly specified part of the whole instrument. And then there was the Solo synthesizer that outperformed every other monophonic synthesizer before or since because it was probably the only keyboard ever sold that offered three modes of touch-sensitivity: velocity, pressure, and side-to-side wiggle. There was also a ribbon controller that allowed you to play the Solo sounds much like a cello or fretless bass. In the whole history of keyboard instruments, nothing had come as close to simulating the nuances of an acoustic instrument. If that were not enough, the GX-1 also offered one of the earliest drum machines ever released, described by one reviewer in January 1976 as "the most realistically voiced electronic drummer I've ever heard." So, three years before the Prophet 5 and Oberheim OBX were to offer a maximum of five and eight voices respectively, the GX-1 offered two independent synthesizer voices for each of the eight notes on its upper manual, two for each of the eight notes on its lower manual, one for the Solo synth, and three for its bass section. That was 36 independent synthesizers, plus a drum machine! It's no wonder that the GX-1 weighed as much as it did. That the whole thing stayed in tune —especially with no auto-tuning capability—was nothing short of miraculous.

Even so, this was far from the end of the story. You could use the GX-1's front panel controls to adjust a vast array of parameters relating to things such as the mix between the Tones in a patch, their pitches, numerous types of modulation, additional filter settings, portamento, reverberation, sustain, and more. Furthermore, the 70 Tone memories were not isolated sounds that you could select only one at a time; you could combine the Tones for each of the upper and lower manuals

and the pedals in 55 ways each, and with a further 10 memories on the Solo synthesizer. That made 175 mixable patch combinations in all.

As you might expect, very few GX-1s saw the shores of Japan receding into the distance. Perhaps the most notorious was Keith Emerson's first, or maybe it was his second, which he bought from John Paul Jones of Led Zeppelin. Stevie Wonder famously used one on *Songs in the Key of Life* and other users were equally prestigious: Benny Andersson of ABBA described his as "without limits," Rick Wright of Pink Floyd had one, as did Hans Zimmer and Jurgen Fritz of Triumvirat. In 1978, former Ekseption keyboard player Rick Van Der Linden even released a solo LP called *GX1*. Oh yes, and the Church of Scientology still has one at its studios in California!

Apparently, Yamaha spent more than $4 million developing the GX-1. This means that, if they sold 50 units (which seems unlikely) at its recommended price, they didn't even recoup their costs. But as far back as 1975, Yamaha's UK demonstrator, Len Rowle, speculated that the GX-1 might be the test bed for a number of new technologies that would find themselves inside other, more modest Yamaha instruments. He was right, and three of these appeared just a year later.

The CS-50 was the baby of the family but, despite offering four-note polyphony (which was a big deal in 1976), it was not a great success. The CS-60 was the next step up. This had double the CS-50's polyphony, and a single memory equivalent to one of the GX-1's Tone memories. Then there was the CS-80, a huge success that dominated the keyboard world for two years from 1976 until 1978. The reason for this was simple. The CS-80 was the direct descendent of the GX-1, with the same dual-voice architecture that made the big, white monster so remarkable. It sounded wonderful and, with its beautifully weighted velocity-sensitive and poly-pressure-sensitive keyboard, the CS-80 remains an unsurpassed performance synthesizer to this day.

It's almost impossible to convey in words the impact that the GX-1 made in the mid-70s. It was not just innovative, but radical in its approach to synthesis. Even today, it's a glorious instrument, and the clear winner of the award for the rarest and most gorgeous production synthesizer of all time. And there's still only one instrument that makes *that* sound.

The Sequential Circuits Prophet 5 (1978)

In 1977, neither of the American keyboard giants of the day offered a true polyphonic synthesizer. Moog had designed the Polymoog around octave-dividing organ technology, and ARP was still experimenting with various incarnations of divide-down technology and "string" synthesis. Yamaha's CS-80 was the successor to the mighty GX-1 but it shared a fundamental failing with its only competitor, the Oberheim 4-Voice: It couldn't store all the parameters that defined a sound. So it was into this immature market that Sequential Circuits (a company that started life in a garage in California) launched its first keyboard instrument, originally called "The Prophet."

The company's founder, Dave Smith, designed this while building a Minimoog programmer and an early digital sequencer and, whether by luck or craft, he hit upon a specification that every keyboard player would soon crave: a five-octave keyboard, genuine polyphony, a powerful polyphonic modulation section, and a punchy sound that was reminiscent of the Minimoog itself.

Based on SSM chips, this synthesizer looked and sounded like the instrument now known universally as the Rev 1 Prophet 5. It differed in just one respect: there were two versions, one that could play five notes at a time, and one that could play 10. Unfortunately, the expanded version was prone to heat build-up and proved to be hopelessly unreliable. The only solution was a radical one: most were changed back to five-voice instruments.

The Prophet 5: no other name rolls off the tongue quite as smoothly. It wasn't just the promise of five programmable voices in a single, polyphonic keyboard, nor the beautiful koa-wood case, the expensive-looking hardware, nor the well-designed control surface; there was a more practical reason why everybody wanted to get their hands on one. It was the first polyphonic synthesizer that could save the value of every parameter in memory. Costing a little under $4,000 at launch (£3,395 in the UK), this made it a marvel; the first polysynth on which you could punch in a patch number and recall the actual sound that you had stored. You can barely imagine the impact that this made.

Unfortunately, early Prophet 5s

keyboard profiles

remained unreliable and required factory modifications to make them useable, but they felt and sounded, in a gloriously indefinable way, just right. But let's get one thing clear: despite the comparison being made ad nauseam, the Prophet was not a polyphonic Minimoog. Its architecture was more closely related to that of an ARP Odyssey than it was to the Moog. The dual oscillators per voice, dedicated LFO, pulse-width modulation, cross modulation, oscillator sync, ADSR envelope generators, and conventional CV and Gate interfaces were all features found on the Odyssey but not on the Minimoog. Nevertheless, the myth flourished.

the market, it continued to offer a depth of sound and facilities that others did not, particularly in the area of modulation. Consequently, a mystique surrounded the Prophet name, and a friend of the author, on a world tour and playing at Madison Square Garden, was refused service in a well-known New York store because he "didn't look like he could afford one." But those who could afford them (and who could get served) eulogized and, for a while, you couldn't avoid the Prophet. Whether your taste ran to Phil Collins' "In the Air Tonight," Paul Hardcastle's "19," Japan's *Tin Drum*, or even the basslines on Madonna's albums, you were listening to Prophet 5s. Then

sound of the instrument escaped almost unscathed. Unfortunately, the word "almost" is important; Rev 3s sounded almost identical to their predecessors, only—in the minds of some players—very slightly less so. Nevertheless, they had many good points including an improved editing system, microtuning capabilities and, on the final version, a leap in memory capacity from 40 to 120 patches.

Sequential released the Prophet's final incarnation, the Rev 3.3, in 1982. Rumors abounded of a later version that offered MIDI as standard, but it seems that all MIDI'd Prophets were retrofitted. Perhaps one of the reasons that the rumor survives is the Prophet Remote, a four-octave sling-on keyboard that you connected to the Prophet using a somewhat unwieldy cable that carried serial data, much as MIDI does today. But the Remote was not a MIDI device, and neither was the synthesizer.

Also in 1982, Sequential launched the Prophet 10. More than simply two Prophet 5s in a dual-manual instrument, this was a monster that could allocate its 10 voices in several modes ranging from a two-oscillator-per-note 10-voice synth, to a monosynth with 20 analog oscillators under a single key. Unfortunately, the Prophet 10 was too expensive to be a great success, whereas the Prophet 5 continued to sweep all before it. With a production run of nearly 6,000 units, the Rev 3s were to become the most successful synths ever produced by Sequential.

Prophet 5 ▲
Saved every parameter in memory

The Rev 1s were hand-assembled, and Smith built only 182 of them before substantially redesigning the Prophet. Externally, the Rev 2 added cassette storage for its patch memories and had a slightly less attractive walnut case but it remained essentially the same instrument. There were eventually to be three subrevisions of this model, called Rev 2.0, 2.1, and 2.2, and Sequential built somewhat over 1,000 of these. For many aficionados, these are the ones to have: relatively reliable, yet retaining the sonic qualities of the earliest models.

By 1980, the Prophet 5 was undoubtedly the synth to own. It sounded fantastic, with a character that was very different from the substantially larger and more temperamental polysynths that had preceded it. Even after competitors started to bring similar instruments to

there were Abba, Dire Straits, Larry Fast, Genesis, Herbie Hancock, Paul McCartney, Pink Floyd, Tangerine Dream, Yes, Led Zeppelin, and more. The user list eventually became an A-list of the 70s and 80s music industry.

By this point, Sequential's reputation was unassailable, even though the Prophet remained unstable and, with fewer than 1,300 yet shipped, difficult to obtain. (The reason for the Prophet's sonic instabilities was to some extent explained by the inherent deficiencies of the SSM chips used. The reason for its rarity was to some extent explained by the inherent deficiencies of the manufacturer of the SSM chips used.) So Smith redesigned it again, this time using CEM chips. This entailed another, much more thorough redesign that included the power supply, envelopes, DACs and VCAs, so it is remarkable that the

For five years, Sequential Circuits flourished. But the world changed in 1983 when Yamaha released the DX7, and the manufacturers of big analog polysynths soon found themselves in deep trouble. ARP had already folded, and Oberheim and Moog were soon to follow. However, Sequential Circuits was made of sterner stuff, and a stream of innovative products kept the company in business for a further four years. The Prophet 600 (1983) was the world's first MIDI synthesizer; the Prophet T8 (also 1983) was a masterpiece of keyboard engineering; the Prophet Six-Trak (1984) was possibly the world's first multi-timbral synthesizer; and the Prophet VS (1986) introduced a new method of sound generation—Vector Synthesis—to the world. But the company never regained the market leadership it had enjoyed from 1978 to 1982, and it finally closed its doors in 1987. The Prophet 5 can be seen on the DVD with this book.

The Fairlight CMI (1979)

In some ways, the Fairlight story began in 1973 with the publication of an Australian magazine called *Electronics Today International*. Publisher Kim Ryrie was interested in sound synthesis and, starting in October 1973, ETI published a series of articles instructing readers how to build two monosynths that were later to reappear in the UK under the Maplin brand name.

Two years later, Ryrie decided to design an analog synthesizer that used digital technology to control its signal path and to store sounds. He contacted an old school friend, electronics designer Peter Vogel and, in 1975, they founded a company called Fairlight, named after a ferry that crosses Sydney harbor. However, they achieved little until they teamed up with a consultant for Motorola named Tony Furse.

Furse had been working independently toward a genuine digital synthesizer, and he had already developed a basic sound generator that used twin Motorola 6800 microprocessors to produce waveforms using a method called additive synthesis. So perhaps it's no surprise that, in 1976, the three unveiled an eight-voice digital synth played from a conventional keyboard, but controlled by a computer's QWERTY keyboard, a monochrome video monitor and a light-pen. Called the QASAR M8, its CPU unit was in keeping with its time: it was large, it was heavy, it was frighteningly complex, and it was ridiculously difficult to build. What's more, those who heard it have since admitted that it sounded pretty awful.

Undeterred, Ryrie and Vogel licensed the Qasar technology from Furse and continued to develop it, taking advantage of the rapid improvements in components throughout the late 70s, and the equally rapid drop in prices. They eventually realized that the Qasar's architecture was unsuitable for commercial production, so they set about redesigning it; in particular, changing the whole architecture of the voice cards. This proved to be the turning point, and the next instrument they unveiled was to change the music industry forever. With two six-octave keyboards, a screen, and another massive processing unit, it was the Fairlight CMI.

The CMI (Computer Musical Instrument) used many of the technologies from the M8, but embodied many advances over it, not least of which was an increase in waveform memory from a total of 4KB to 16KB for each of its eight voices. (Its total memory of 128KB was, at the time, a massive amount of RAM.) The consequence of this was that, instead of being limited to storing and replaying static waveforms, the CMI was capable of replaying eight complete sounds, albeit short ones by today's standards. Apparently, Ryrie and Vogel didn't much like this idea at first, but they nonetheless added an input board that could record external sounds, allowing them to be saved to the huge 8-inch diskettes that the CMI used. Sampling had arrived.

Introduced in 1979, the CMI was first demonstrated in Britain on the BBC's popular technology program, *Tomorrow's World*. This provoked a huge amount of interest, and although the cost was high (around $25,000 in the US) Peter Gabriel immediately obtained one and then helped to establish a UK importer, Syco Systems. Syco then supplied instruments to John Paul Jones of Led Zeppelin and to Kate Bush, whose fourth album, *The Dreaming*, was virtually a showcase for the CMI. In little more than a year, Fairlight leapt from an unknown name to the pinnacle of the keyboard world.

The original CMI was produced for two years until it was superseded in 1982 by a significantly improved and more powerful version, the Series II. This offered a higher sampling frequency (which dramatically improved the sound quality) and introduced the famous Page R, which was perhaps the first pattern-based sequencer to be made available within a commercial product. On its own, Page R might not have had much impact but, because each of the voice boards had its own RAM, it was possible to store different sounds on each, allowing users to replay multiple sounds as well as multiple notes simultaneously. If users placed, say, a kick drum sample on board 1, a snare drum on board 2, hi-hats on board 3, a bass guitar sample on voice 4, and so on, Page R allowed them to sequence and replay complete tracks on the CMI alone. Since the sequencer was grid-based, these tracks were very rigid and mechanical, which some musicians hated. Others, however, took the technology to heart, and with the CMI in the hands of producers such as

Trevor Horn, players including Thomas Dolby and bands such as Frankie Goes to Hollywood, Depeche Mode, Human League, and the Pet Shop Boys, electro-pop was born.

The last version of the "classic" eight-bit Fairlights appeared in 1983. The Series IIx was based upon the newer, more powerful Motorola 6809 processors, and added MIDI and SMPTE timecode capabilities. In addition to the improved hardware, the IIx included much improved software with 20 pages of menus offering everything from simple housekeeping to detailed control over all aspects of the hardware, from additive synthesis to sampling, and from composing using MCL (the Music Composition Language) to real-time sequencing.

Between 1979 and 1984, approximately 300 Fairlights were built, of which around 50 were shipped to the company's best market: the UK. However, it's not possible to say how many of each model now exist because it was possible to upgrade the older ones by replacing their voice cards, by retrospectively adding the MIDI and SMPTE facilities, and so on.

By this time, the Fairlight was as much a mainstay of the industry as, say, the Mellotron had been in the 1960s, or string machines had been in the 1970s, and many of its samples were on the verge of becoming musical clichés; none more so than the orchestral hit called ORCH5. And, as with all classic instruments, the reason for this was a simple one: the CMI sounded fantastic. However, technological advances were appearing at ever-shorter intervals and, by the time that the IIx entered the market, processor and memory prices were tumbling at a remarkable rate. By the end of 1984, the cheaper E-mu Systems Emulator and Emulator II had stolen a large part of Fairlight's professional market, and truly low-cost samplers such as the Ensoniq Mirage were already on the horizon. So, just a year after its introduction, Fairlight ditched the 8-bit Series IIx and replaced it with the 16-bit Series III. This was an altogether more advanced product, designed for use in movie production and other high-end applications, and it had a high-end price to match; up to $100,000, depending upon configuration.

The Series III signaled the end of Fairlight's love affair with the music industry, and the start of its evolution through multiple bankruptcies and reincarnations into a manufacturer of hard disk systems for film production and broadcast. But it is for the CMI that the name Fairlight will be most fondly remembered. Sure, its samples were only eight-bit and of limited bandwidth, but it had a sonic depth and authority that has never quite been emulated, and although surviving units are outperformed in every way by modern synthesizers and samplers, there is still something a bit special about a Fairlight.

The Yamaha DX7 (1983)

The history of the DX7 begins at the Bell Telephone Laboratories in the 1950s, where a gentleman by the name of Max Matthews had begun to experiment with digital computers to see whether they could generate audio signals. Matthews was far ahead of his time because he realized that—unlike the primitive analog signal generators of the time—computer-generated digital audio could be consistent and controllable.

In 1957, Matthews wrote a program called MUSIC I that ran on an IBM mainframe computer. This was capable only of generating basic sounds but Matthews continued his developments and MUSIC II, MUSIC III, and, by 1967, three versions of MUSIC IV had appeared.

Elsewhere, in Stanford University's computer department, researchers John Chowning and Leland Smith were working on another version of the MUSIC program. Chowning was also experimenting with vibrato, applying this to the audio frequency signals generated by the digital oscillators within the program. Apocrypha has it that he accidentally programmed a vibrato that was faster and deeper than he had intended, discovering that the result was not vibrato, but a tone unlike anything that he had heard before. He had stumbled across a common technique used to broadcast radio transmissions: frequency modulation of a carrier signal by a modulator. But, by modulating an audio signal, he became the first person to hear what we now call FM synthesis.

Chowning continued to develop FM, adding functions that allowed him to control the sounds he created. Then, in 1971, Matthews suggested to him that he should create a range of conventional sounds such as organs or brass to demonstrate that FM was a possible basis for a commercial keyboard. Chowning did so, and persuaded Stanford's Office of

Technology Licensing to approach companies for him. Hammond and Wurlitzer turned Stanford away, but Yamaha despatched a young engineer to meet Chowning. After a brief evaluation, Yamaha negotiated a one-year license to investigate FM and, in 1973, it began development of a prototype FM monosynth.

Surprisingly, Yamaha's efforts did not lead to the world's first commercial FM synthesizer. Called the Synclavier, this was announced by the New England Digital Corporation in 1978, and was a polyphonic synthesizer based upon 8-bit FM and additive synthesis. So, despite its head start, it was not until 1981 that Yamaha unveiled its first FM synths. The GS1 (which looked like a miniature grand piano) and GS2 forsook recognized elements such as oscillators and filters, and instead incorporated frightening new concepts such as multi-operator equation generators, 30kHz data rates, and digital-to-analog converters.

The operation of these expensive machines was a complete mystery to all but the most mathematically oriented, but that didn't matter. Neither instrument allowed players to edit its sounds, each being capable only of playing the 500-odd voices supplied by Yamaha on little magnetic "lollypop" sticks. Yet they sounded great, and Toto, for example, layered nearly a dozen tracks of GS1 on million-selling hits such as "Rosanna" and "Africa."

In 1982, Yamaha released the first low-cost FM keyboards, the CE-20 and CE-25. Combining monophonic voices, polyphonic sounds and ensemble, these were revolutionary, but their cosmetic design aimed them squarely at the home keyboard market, so they created very little stir in professional circles. But the same year, the company demonstrated a keyboard with "equation generators" that you could edit. Never released in its original form, it was the progenitor of one of the most important synthesizers ever created: the DX7.

Despite its decade-long gestation, the first batch of DX7s proved to be a bit of a problem because, just as they entered production, Sequential Circuits launched the Prophet 600—the world's first MIDI synth. The prototype DX7 had no MIDI, so Yamaha quickly modified it to transmit and receive on MIDI channel 1. Despite these teething troubles, the DX7 was an instant sensation: its editable FM engine allowed programmers to create sounds of unprecedented complexity, and its 16-voice polyphony made a mockery of the 5-note and 8-note analog synths of the era. It offered 32 patch memories, and you could use its groundbreaking ROM and RAM cartridges to expand the number of sounds available. Furthermore, breath control augmented its velocity and aftertouch-sensitivity. Then there was the price: at just $2,000, the DX7 was very affordable.

It soon became clear that the DX7's forté was percussive instruments and anything that sounded like two bits of metal being banged against each other. It also excelled at orchestral imitations such as brass and woodwind. But in stark contrast to its sonic capabilities, the DX7 looked surprisingly conservative. At a time when many keyboards sported multicolored control panels, Yamaha had given the DX7 a slim, sober, and professional appearance that was in stark contrast to its breathtaking palette of new sounds, many of which remain classics to this day. Of these, the now clichéd DX7 electric piano patch is probably the most (in)famous, and it shows no sign of disappearing. Indeed, it is so popular that it has become almost impossible to buy an electronic piano or a polyphonic synthesizer without an imitative patch named "DX Piano" or something similar.

However, just as the DX7 had great strengths, it also had weaknesses. It was unable to create the warm pads that were the meat and drink of any self-respecting analog polysynth, it was incapable of the characteristic filter

▲ **Yamaha DX7** he DX7 excelled at percussion, brass, and woodwind sounds.

keyboard facts

sweeps that dominated (and still dominate) much of popular music, and its achievements in the field of lead synthesis were, to be polite, less than memorable.

It also had functional disabilities. It wasn't long before players noticed the hiss generated by early models, that it was a MIDI imbecile, and that it suffered from the most obnoxious operating system ever devised for a commercial keyboard. Indeed, FM synthesis was simply too much science for players brought up on VCOs, VCFs, and VCAs. Far from being, as Yamaha claimed, "an easier synthesizer to program than ever before," it precluded most players from all but the most serendipitous prodding, and many elected to use it as a preset instrument. Consequently, a whole support industry was established, fueling players' desires for more memories, more sounds, a better MIDI implementation, arpeggiators, and even computer-based patch editors for the brave.

The DX7 had taken the world by storm, and it quickly became the biggest-selling synthesizer of all time. In just four years, it sold a dozen times as many units as the Minimoog had in 13, and it dominated the keyboard market as no synthesizer had ever done before. It also spawned an immense dynasty, including the DX1, which was perhaps the greatest FM synthesizer of them all, plus dozens of other DXs, TXs, YSs, SYs, and more.

Then there were the innumerable home keyboards, digital pianos, monstrous 3-manual organs, tiny sound modules, and even PC sound cards. But in 1987, the reign of the DX7 ended quite abruptly. Direct descendents of the DX7 such as the DX7/IID, DX7/IIFD, and DX7S, while good instruments in their own rights, recaptured neither the public's imagination nor the magic of the original. It was time for something new. The DX7 features on the DVD.

The Roland D-50 (1987)

The Yamaha DX7 and its siblings had dominated the keyboard market throughout the mid 1980s. Previous industry leaders had been unable to keep pace with either the low prices or the facilities offered by FM-based instruments, and revered manufacturers such as ARP, Moog, and the original Oberheim had already disappeared by the middle of the

decade. Across the Pacific, a handful of Japanese manufacturers were faring better than their American counterparts, but even the best-known of these, Roland and Korg, were lagging behind, offering analog/digital hybrids such as the Super-JX10 and the DW-8000. In short, FM synthesis was king, and the rest of the keyboard world was in the doldrums.

But behind the scenes, Roland's engineers had been developing a number of new technologies, and 1986 was to see an explosion of innovative products. These included a remarkable family of "HP" digital pianos (the descendents of which are still, according to many players, the best available) and a series of samplers that, for a while, set the standard for such instruments. But as far as performance synthesizers were concerned, Roland still lagged behind Yamaha.

It therefore came as a surprise when, in 1987, the company announced an entirely new type of synthesizer. It was an immediate sensation, and the company's demos stunned listeners almost as much as the first Mellotrons and Minimoogs had, years before.

Superficially, the D-50 didn't look remarkable. Sleek and stylish, certainly, but it was still a five-octave synthesizer with a small screen and bunch of buttons and sliders on its control panel. So, what made it special?

One reason was its method of synthesis, which Roland called "Linear Arithmetic" or "LA" synthesis. The company's engineers had discovered that much of the information that humans use to identify a sound is contained in its first few hundred milliseconds. They reasoned, therefore, that synthesized sounds would be more realistic if snippets of "real" instruments were placed before the conventional synthesis waveforms. Consequently, the D-50 contained a ROM that held 100 PCM samples. Although these were very short by today's standards, they enabled the D-50 to produce imitative sounds that were far more interesting and convincing than any previous synthesizer, as well as a completely new palette of sounds that nobody had ever heard before.

Another reason for the D-50's success was its inclusion of internal effects—chorus plus 32 different types of delay and reverb—which made it the first performance synth to sound expensively "produced" without the need for outboard equipment. In

addition, the D-50's keyboard was both velocity- and aftertouch-sensitive, the synth engine offered numerous algorithms for building sounds in different ways, and its many combinations of splits, layers, and mono-modes made it enormously flexible. But fundamentally, there was a single overpowering reason why the D-50 was a sensation, instantly toppling the DX7 from the throne it had occupied unchallenged for four years. It sounded fantastic.

At first sight, the D-50 seemed quite complex to edit; not as impenetrable as the DX7 perhaps, but not straightforward either. So, to assist players who found the onboard programming system a little daunting, Roland offered an analog-style control surface, the PG1000. Once this was attached, it quickly became obvious that, although the D50 was digital throughout, it was in many ways an analog-style synthesizer with a conventional architecture of oscillators, filters, envelopes, and so on. This meant that Roland had avoided the trap into which Yamaha had fallen with its arcane FM programming system. The D-50 made digital synthesis accessible again.

The enormous popularity of the D-50 soon caused a whole industry to spring up around it. Roland had had the foresight to equip it with external sockets for ROM and RAM cards, an advanced MIDI implementation, and even the ability to host internal expansion boards that extended the range of sounds and facilities on offer. This meant that third-party manufacturers could develop voice cards for it, as well as software libraries, powerful editors, and more. For many owners, it became unnecessary to learn how to program the instrument; they simply plugged in their favorite sounds and played.

Almost inevitably, as had happened in 1980 with the Fairlight's cello and choir samples, and again in 1983 with the DX7's electric pianos, the D-50 nearly crossed the line from overnight success to overnight cliché. It wasn't only established players such as Nick Rhodes, Jean Michel Jarre, Gary Numan, Kitaro, and Rick Wakeman who were using them: its factory sounds suddenly appeared on almost every soundtrack and in every lift around the world. In particular, patch 11, "Fantasia" was everywhere, and this became such a classic that variations on it featured on every subsequent Roland synthesizer, and it has since been imitated on almost every sample-based workstation released by other manufacturers. Other instantly recognizable D-50 sounds included Soundtrack, OK Chorale, and Nightmare, while imitations of Glass Voices and Intruder FX have become a staple of all modern synths, as have copies of DigitalNativeDance, which introduced another type of sound, wave sequencing, to the public consciousness. But few if any of these copies—whether from Roland or elsewhere—approached the warmth and depth of the originals. The D-50 had a unique character that remained unequalled until the company recreated the whole synthesizer in software for its V-Synth and V-Synth XT products, launched in 2004.

Within six months of shipping the D-50, Roland released the MT-32 module, which was designed for home use alongside an electronic piano or home keyboard. Unlike the D-50 and its modular equivalent the D-550 (which could combine four PCM or synthesized "partials" within a single patch) the MT-32 only offered two partials per patch, and its sound was thinner and less involving.

The following year, the company released its D-10 and D-20 keyboards. The D-20 was another milestone, being the first affordable instrument to combine multi-timbral sound generation, percussion samples, a multi-track sequencer, digital effects, and a floppy disk drive for sound and song storage. These were then followed by the D-110 rackmount module and, in 1989, the last of the series, the D-5. All of these employed the limited form of LA synthesis pioneered by the MT-32 so, in comparison to the D-50, they sounded uniformly uninspiring. Nevertheless, they were hugely popular, eventually becoming the most successful synthesizers yet released by the company.

In 1990, Roland discontinued the D-50 and replaced it with the D-70. Advertised as the "Super-LA" synthesizer, this promised much, and featured a unique programming feature called DLM (Differential Loop Modulation) that made some really off-the-wall sounds possible. But the D-70 lacked the appeal of the D-50, and it was not a great success. Fortunately, Super-LA paved the way for the synthesis engine in the JD-800 keyboard (which became a classic in its own right) and thereafter for the huge "JV" family of synthesizers and

modules, the "XV" modules, and the Fantom synthesizers of the present day.

Consequently, the legacy of the D-50 is very much with us. Every time you play a PCM-based keyboard—whether from Roland, Yamaha, Korg, or a host of other manufacturers—you should tip your hat in its direction.

The Korg M1 (1987)

By the mid 80s, the idea of combining a sample-based sound generator, percussion sounds, and sequencing in a single instrument was no longer radical. The Fairlight CMI had pioneered the idea of the all-in-one keyboard in the late 1970s, and the Synclavier had pursued a similar course based primarily around FM synthesis. Players could create multiple sounds simultaneously on both of these instruments, and use their onboard sequencers to create compositions, albeit with a limited number of notes available at any given time. However, the technical limitations of the day meant that no track composed and played entirely on a Fairlight or Synclavier was ever going to sound polished unless the facilities of a recording studio were available to apply effects, final EQ, and so on. Furthermore, their very high prices ensured that they would never be mass-market products, and you were never going to see one being played in your local pub.

Then, in 1987, Roland brought another new technology to the keyboard world. The D50, as well as being one of the first synthesizers to use short samples as the basis of its sound generation, was also the first to incorporate digital reverb processors within the keyboard itself. So the next step was inevitable: somebody was going to combine the ideas of the synthesizer/sequencer with the synthesizer/effects processor to create the first synthesizer workstation. Launched in 1988, the Roland D20 combined everything players needed to create complete compositions, but it was not a great-sounding synthesizer. All the plaudits were (and still are) offered to the keyboard that followed.

For much of the 1980s, Korg had been in the doldrums. Yamaha had found dozens of ways to repackage FM synthesis and maintain its huge market share. Elsewhere, Casio's CZ-series ruled the low-cost end of the market, and previously mighty companies such as Sequential Circuits were heading the

same way as Moog, ARP, and Oberheim into liquidation. Korg—once a major innovator of monosynths, multi-keyboards and unusual polysynths—was nowhere near the head of the market, and its existing range of DSS samplers, low-cost FM polysynths, and analog/digital hybrids was no match for its competition. Something had to be done, and it was. In a single, mighty leap, Korg pioneered the use of VLSI (very large scale integration) chip technology in synthesizers, and increased the power of their products way beyond the LSI technology of its competitors. Pouring all their expertise into a single groundbreaking instrument, the company's engineers created the M1 and in the summer of 1988 this didn't just shake the synthesizer world. It redefined it.

Unlike Roland's D-series, the M1's "AI" sound engine did not use tiny snippets of samples. Instead, it offered a huge (at the time) 4MB ROM with extended and looped samples that could be used to create never-before heard sounds as well as imitative patches that had escaped even the best synthesizers of previous years: expressive saxophones, Mellotron-esque choral ensembles, and convincing guitars, to name but three. Its programming system was also a revelation, very analog in structure, and accessible to anybody who had mastered a synthesizer in the 70s and early 80s. Even if you didn't want to learn to program sounds, the M1 was a fabulous tool, and factory patches such as Univers, Ooh/Ahh, Pole, and Lore were soon to be heard flooding the airwaves.

The M1 excelled in other areas too. Although limited by modern standards, its MIDI sequencer was unrecognizable from the primitive Page "R" of the Fairlight, and it offered a degree of flexibility only previously associated with computer-based software. In addition, its digital effects section dramatically extended the range and flexibility of effects available, adding phasing, flanging, delay, distortion, overdrive, and excitation (among others) to the basic chorus and reverb found on the Rolands. It was also expandable, with a slot for PCM cards that increased the number of waveforms available, and a second that accepted ROM and RAM cards for storing additional banks of sounds and performances. As had happened for the DX7 and the D-50, a miniature industry sprung up around the M1, and soon there were numerous MIDI editors and librarians available for it, plus patch libraries, programming guides, and more.

But perhaps the most significant leap forward was in the variety of ways in which players could allocate its 16 voices across its five-octave velocity- and aftertouch-sensitive keyboard. Three different modes of operation offered up to eight simultaneous patches, and these could be layered, split, cross-faded, velocity-faded, or simultaneously driven from up to eight independent MIDI channels.

Launched in 1988, the M1 was as much of a sensation as the D-50 had been the year before. Indeed, commentators of the time described it as an "eight-part multi-timbral D-50" because it had a similar, polished sound, and it soon found favor with bands such as The Pet Shop Boys, Depeche Mode, The Orb, and The KLF.

But the M1 was not just an improved "S&S" (sample and synthesis) synthesizer; its architecture laid down a template for the keyboard workstation that has never been replaced. Enhanced, yes (and it was Korg who would come up with the next big step forward in 1995) but never replaced. Consequently, just as the D-50 had toppled the DX7 from its throne, the M1 became the keyboard of choice and, at a stroke, it established Korg as the leading workstation manufacturer, a position that it has held ever since.

Within a year, the M1 was on the way to become the best-selling synthesizer of all time, and had spawned a family of AI-based keyboards and sound modules. The M1 itself was distilled into a 2U rackmount module, the M1R, and there was a low-cost, cut-down version with half the sound generation system, the M3R. At the other end of the scale, Korg didn't just stick larger keyboards on the M1 to create 76- and 88-note versions; they expanded its ROM to create the T3 (61-note), T2 (76-note) and T1 (88-note) workstations.

In addition, there were "EX" expansions that enhanced many of the models still further, and boards that enabled the larger T-series keyboards to sample sounds and use these alongside the internal PCMs.

Other manufacturers quickly copied the M1 formula, and Korg soon faced stiff competition from the likes of the Roland JV-1000, itself a very fine workstation that would eventually

evolve into the Roland workstations available today. So, in 1992, Korg announced the "01W" range (a strange name that has caused some people to wonder whether it was actually designed as the "M10") and, later, there were the X- and N-series, which refined the "AI" concept still further, adding new programming and sequencing capabilities plus massive new sound

Korg M1
The M1 remains a classic to this day.

memories, albeit in lower-cost hardware.

Nevertheless, it was the M1 that had set the standard, and it remained in production until 1994, simply because people still wanted to buy a genuine M1 rather than the more powerful and ostensibly better-sounding instruments that superseded it. To this day, it remains a classic.

The Clavia Nord Lead (1994)

In 1994, Yamaha unveiled a family of synthesizers that—had they released them all—might have changed the face of synthesis as radically as the DX7 had, 11 years before. Initially, there were to be two instruments. The first was a duophonic, soloing synth called the VL1; the second was a polysynth called the VP1.

The VL1 introduced a technology that is now so commonplace that we sometimes forget how remarkable it was in the mid-90s. This was "physical modeling," in which the characteristics of existing instruments are analyzed and broken down into mathematical models, and then reconstructed in virtual form using digital signal processing. The system in the VL1 was called S/VA (Self-oscillating Virtual Acoustic) synthesis and, like the Frequency Modulation (FM) synthesis on which the DX7 was based, it was licensed from Stanford University in the U.S. While S/VA offered a limited number of recognizable features such

as envelopes and a filter, it introduced a whole new vocabulary of terms for synthesists: pressure, embouchure, tonguing, scream, and throat formant, to name but a few. Unfortunately, this meant that few programmers could get to grips with the VL1, especially since is only revealed its true quality when played using a breath controller, which is a skill that few keyboard players have ever mastered.

Alongside the VL1, the VP1 uses a somewhat different form of modeling called F/VA (Free-oscillation Virtual Acoustic) synthesis, and Yamaha claimed that this would be more suited to the generation of polyphonic timbres. Many commentators speculated that this would be the more interesting of the two new synths, possibly leading to the demise of PCM-based (S&S) synthesis! However, something strange happened. The VL1 begat a more affordable (although somewhat cut-down) version, the VL7, and a small family of rackmount modules but, despite being lauded as "the next big thing" by many reviewers, it sold poorly. No matter . . . Yamaha has a long history of releasing pioneering instruments that would later spawn affordable descendents: for example, the GX-1 begat the CS-series, the GS-1 begat the DX-series, and so on. But where was the VP1? It wasn't vaporware, because prototypes were spotted, but it was never released and, despite leading the world in the new technology of physical modeling, Yamaha for once failed to capitalize on its advantage.

The story now jumps from Japan to Sweden, where a much smaller company (tiny, in fact) had avoided all the pitfalls that caused the VL1 to be less than a huge commercial success. Firstly, and most obviously, the VL1 was far too expensive to appeal to a wide market. Secondly, S/VA was too arcane, and few players had the inclination to get to grips with it. Thirdly, it produced the wrong sounds. Sure, it sounded superb, but few people wanted their keyboards to produce better imitations of saxophones or correctly tongued trumpets; most wanted them to create better "synthesizer" sounds. The solution was obvious; instead of modeling blown and bowed instruments, why not model an analog synthesizer? And then, having done so, why not control the model using a one-knob-per-function control panel that used names such as waveform, resonance, modulation amount, and all the other instantly recognizable terms of traditional synthesis? If the results could be made affordable, it seemed more than likely that this "virtual analog" (VA) synthesis would be of interest. So this is what the Swedes did. The company—previously known only for its ddrums digital percussion—was Clavia, and the synthesizer was the Nord Lead.

The Nord Lead was launched 1995 and, like the Prophet 5, the DX7, and the M1, its concepts shook the keyboard world to its foundations. Not that this was apparent at the time: indeed, some people questioned why— given the availability of the "real" thing—a digital recreation of an analog synthesizer was needed. But this was shortsighted. The cost of digital technology was dropping rapidly, and while the Nord Lead generated just four voices, it was obvious that the number of voices would climb quickly and that the price would drop almost as swiftly. What's more, it was inevitable that the accuracy and flexibility of the VSM (Virtual Sound Modeling) analog models would improve rapidly. Then there were other factors such as the reliability of DSP-based synthesizers, their compact size, their lightness, and their upgradeability. It was going to be a digital future, and Clavia grasped it with both hands.

The Nord Lead remained in production for three years but, although its software was revised to version two in 1996, its hardware was already proving to be a limitation. So, in 1998, the company replaced it with the more powerful Nord Lead 2, which added more voices, more filters, and more outputs to the original specification. This was then joined in 2001 by the Nord Lead 3, and both models were manufactured side-by-side from 2001 to 2003, whereupon the "2" was discontinued. Happily, all three models proved to be commercial and artistic successes, eventually boasting users such as Fatboy Slim, Nine Inch Nails, The Prodigy, and Autechre, all of whom seemed happy to be seen with these bright red little synths. And why not? They were simple to use, they were reliable, and they sounded great.

Capitalizing upon their understanding of virtual analog synthesis, Clavia launched a second family of products called the Nord Modular in 1997. There were two of these, plus a Micro Modular, and in

2003, the Nord Modular G2. If the original Nord Lead was in many ways a "virtual" Prophet 5, the Modulars were "virtual" modular synthesizers, offering users the freedom to connect and experiment with digital recreations of modules such as oscillators, filters, contour generators, and all the other building blocks of analog synthesis.

Not long after the Nord Lead appeared, the market started to fill up with alternatives. Just three months later, Korg announced two keyboards based upon physical modeling and virtual analog synthesis. Like Yamaha, the company split these into two families, starting with the monophonic Prophecy and the polyphonic OASYS, a keyboard that—like the Yamaha VP1— never appeared in its proposed form. These offered numerous physical models, some recreating acoustic instruments, still more recreating numerous forms of analog and existing digital synthesis methods.

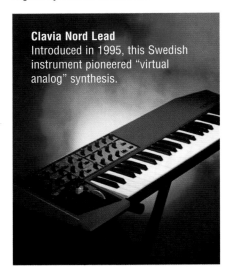

Clavia Nord Lead
Introduced in 1995, this Swedish instrument pioneered "virtual analog" synthesis.

Elsewhere, other manufacturers' products forsook the acoustic modeling and concentrated only on virtual analog synthesis. Early examples of these included Roland's JP-8000 and JP-8080, the Oberheim OB-12, and perhaps the most highly rated of the early "VA" synths, the Access Virus. Even Yamaha tried its hand again, with the underrated AN1X. Nevertheless, it was Clavia who first traveled the virtual analog path and, small though it is, the company has remained for more than a decade one of the major manufacturers of such instruments. Of course, VA synthesis never replaced genuine analog synthesizers, any more than S/VA synthesis replaced real saxophones, but virtual analog synths now offer sound generation and modulation facilities, numbers of

voices, and onboard effects about which genuine analog synths can barely dream. As predicted, the world changed, but it was little Clavia that had led the way, not the mighty Yamaha Corporation.

The Korg Trinity (1995)

When it launched the Trinity in the UK in July 1995, Korg was very clever in its choice of venue, hiring the Science Museum in London. As a result, the press and other observers were already primed (consciously or not) for something special. The company did not disappoint, announcing not one but three radical new keyboards: the Trinity, the Prophecy, and the prototype of the original OASYS, the last of which would never be seen again.

During the launch demonstration, it became clear that—despite being another sample-based workstation— there was something special about the Trinity. Perhaps its appearance should have given us an inkling of this; in an era of predominantly black synthesizers with small LED screens, the Trinity was radically silver, with brushed aluminium panels and silver-colored mouldings, and it boasted a large LCD. More importantly, it was apparent that the sound quality and flexibility of the Trinity's ACCESS sound generator was superior to anything heard before. This was the first of Korg's workstation engines to incorporate resonant filters (itself a huge leap forward) and there were so many PCM multi-samples in its ROM that its program memory was insufficient to take advantage of all of them.

The Trinity was also the first keyboard workstation to offer a touch-sensitive screen as its major control interface. Now commonplace, this was radical in 1995; simply touch a parameter name or the icon for a knob or fader, and then edit it using all manner of controls, or even by dragging your finger across the screen. This significantly simplified programming and user-control, and was a huge benefit when compared with the multiple control sections and increasingly complex menu structures of other workstations.

The next innovation was equally radical: the Trinity offered a hard disk recorder option, the HDR-TRI. Digital recording already existed on hyper-expensive systems such as the Synclavier, and it's something that we now take for granted on workstations, but the Trinity was the instrument that first integrated MIDI sequencing and hard disk recording in an affordable environment. In retrospect, the Trinity's system was not a replacement for a complete computer-based studio, but if you wanted to spin guitars, vocals, and other acoustic sounds into your MIDI compositions, you could do so with ease, taking full advantage of the Trinity's automated mixer, dedicated EQs, and effects sends and returns. As a bonus, the HDR-TRI expansion also allowed players to use the Trinity as a signal processor, playing external audio through the synth's extensive range of effects processes.

Korg had promised many other ways to expand the Trinity and, shortly after the keyboard went on sale, the company released a multi-channel (ADAT) digital I/O board (the DI-TRI), a hard disk interface (the SCSI-TRI) that improved upon the built-in floppy drive, and a flash memory expansion (the PBS-TRI) that made it possible to load Akai and Korg sample libraries. What's more, with the exception of the most basic 61-note version, three of the four models—the 61-note Trinity Plus, the 76-note Trinity Pro, and the 88-note Trinity Pro X—included as standard the physical modeling sound generator from the Korg Prophecy monosynth. With nine distinct methods of physical modeling synthesis, this board (the SOLO-TRI) turned the Trinity into a superb monosynth, and allowed players to add accurate and expressive solo instruments, powerful lead-synths, and bass sounds to their compositions.

But if the touch screen was innovative and extremely useful (which it was), and the expansion options were exciting (which they were), and the physical modeling board put the Trinity in a different league (which it did), they all came second to the Trinity's new effects architecture. The problem with all previous workstations (and many that have been released since) was that, despite being able to generate many different sounds simultaneously, these all passed down the same internal signal paths and through the same effects processors. This meant that if you wanted to apply (say) overdrive and delay to a lead guitar patch, you couldn't apply chorus to the bass guitar, nor gated reverb to the snare drum, nor a rotary speaker effect to the organ, and so on. The Trinity changed all of that because you could allocate its eight Insert effects freely to individual sounds, which

meant that it was the first truly multi-timbral keyboard workstation. Inevitably, a finite amount of processing power meant there were limitations to the number of effects you could apply if you wanted to use the more complex algorithms. Nonetheless, with up to 10 simultaneous, independent effects units (including two Master effects sections), the Trinity was the first workstation that allowed players to create studio-quality tracks without recourse to external processors. Finally, to allow players to get the most from everything on offer, all the Trinity models boasted superb keyboards; expensive Yamaha mechanisms that were far more playable and responsive than the lower-cost Fatar keyboards installed in other Korg products of the era.

Not surprisingly, the Trinity was a huge success, reinforcing Korg's position as the leading manufacturer of keyboard workstations. For a while, it seemed that almost every keyboard player was standing behind a rig that included at least one of these very recognizable silver beasties, and its user-list quickly became a "who's who" of the mid 90s, ranging from Deep Forest and Orbital at one end of the spectrum to Dream Theater and David Bowie at the other.

Nonetheless, Korg wasn't resting on its laurels and, in 1997, it released a low-cost rackmount version of the Trinity, the TR-Rack. This retained the ACCESS sound engine, lost a number of features (such as the touch screen and the sequencer) that were inappropriate for a module, and gained additional banks of sounds and PCM samples, plus a PC interface and a computer-based editor. Then, in 1998, an enhanced keyboard version appeared. The Trinity V3 substituted an enhanced six-voice synthesizer (the MOSS-TRI board) for the SOLO-TRI board of the earlier models and, in effect, added a version of Korg's superb Z1 polyphonic, physical modeling synthesizer to the Trinity. Happily, it was simple to upgrade any existing Trinity to a V3, simply by replacing the older expansion board with the newer (which took just minutes) and then loading the new software that came with it.

Nevertheless, it was only a year until the Trinity range was superseded by the Korg Triton, in which the ACCESS sound engine was replaced by Korg's new HI (Hyper Integrated) sound generator. For users acquainted with the Trinity, it was simple to adapt

to the Triton's new facilities and control menus. Furthermore, there seemed to be more of just about everything on offer, plus the very significant bonus of expansion slots to add new sample sets to the onboard PCM sounds. But for some players, a little bit of the magic had been lost. The Triton was a hugely powerful instrument and, commercially, it took up where the Trinity left off, eventually being repackaged as the KARMA workstation, the Triton Studio, the Triton LE (2001), and the Triton Extreme (2004). In all its guises, the Triton would prove to be a very successful product line but, for some, the Trinity was a classic that has yet to be superseded.

The Korg OASYS (2005)

After the launch of the Korg Trinity, the keyboard world entered a decade of consolidation. Workstations became ever more powerful, but the basic pattern remained largely unchanged: a dedicated VLSI processor provided the power for a core of sample-based synthesis augmented by a selection of other synthesis types married to a wide selection of effects, sequencing and (at the top of the range) hard disk recording. To be fair, Roland extended the boundaries of sound generation in 2000 with its Variphrase technology, and the V-Synth (2003) was an exceptional synthesizer, but it was perhaps not the revolution that the company had hoped. The real action lay elsewhere: to be specific, it was happening on our personal computers.

As far back as the 1970s, companies had been using microprocessors and their associated electronics to create sounds. The Fairlight CMI had been based upon the Motorola 6800 and was later upgraded in its Series IIx incarnation to the 6809 chips used in early video arcade games as well as short-lived home computers such as the Dragon. Similarly, the Fairlight Series III used the Motorola 68000 that lay at the heart of the Atari ST range and the earliest Apple Macs. It was therefore inevitable that developers would look at microcomputers as potential sound generators. Attractive though this idea was, there were many problems to be overcome, the principal of which was the fact that most operating systems are not designed for real-time use, so it takes a great deal of care to ensure that audio can be generated without glitches. Nonetheless, the increasing power of the central processors, the availability of huge amounts of cheap RAM and disk space, and the addition of fast communication protocols such as USB eventually made "software synthesizers" practical. As the world moved into the 21st century, there was an explosion of such products, and we entered the era of the softsynth.

Amazingly, most softsynths sought not to extend the boundaries of sound generation but to imitate revered analog instruments such as Mellotrons, Rhodes pianos, Minimoogs, and Prophets. Then somebody had the bright idea of placing a conventional PC motherboard inside the case of a music keyboard, allowing users to launch commercial softsynths within something that looked like, and felt somewhat like, a keyboard workstation. It was an interesting concept, but these products were hampered by numerous shortcomings, not least of which was the unreliability of the PCs and Microsoft Windows operating systems at their cores. Roland experimented with a variation of the idea, developing the VariOS, a module that promised to host numerous, dedicated software synthesizers, but only three packages were ever released for the system so it was not a success. So now we turn back to Korg, and to a development that had been launched alongside the Trinity in 1995, but never released in its original form: the OASYS.

In the early 1990s, Korg had been developing physical modeling on a platform called SynthKit. The OASYS (Open Architecture SYnthesis System) was to have been a polyphonic instrument that would allow users to load different physical models, assign them to areas of the keyboard or to velocity ranges, and to use them simultaneously. Unfortunately, it was too far ahead of its time, and its hardware was incapable of supporting the concept. Apart from a few appearances at trade shows and press events the OASYS was never seen, and the prototype soon disappeared back into the bowels of Korg, never to emerge again.

Two years later, some of the polyphonic models developed for the OASYS found their way into the Korg

Z1 polysynth and, a few years later, a product called the OASYS PCI appeared. However, this had turned the idea on its head: instead of being a synthesizer with a computer inside, it was a synthesizer board that you installed inside a computer. Unfortunately, this still suffered from some severe limitations—most notably low polyphony—and it was not the groundbreaking product that its developers had hoped.

Then, in January 2005, Korg announced the third generation of the OASYS (now called the Open Architecture SYnthesis Studio) and, unlike the first two incarnations, this proved to be everything that the original concept had promised, and more.

Physically, the OASYS was beautiful, and it exuded quality. Its 76- and 88-note keyboards returned to the high quality of the original Trinities, the

▲ **Korg OASYS**

control ergonomics were first-class, and its 10.4-inch color, touch-sensitive screen showed that Korg had taken a big step beyond the existing crop of workstations.

Nevertheless, the real news was inside its case. The heart of the OASYS was a 2.8GHz Pentium-4 PC that, instead of running Microsoft Windows, ran a core operating system based on Linux, which was itself derived from the Unix operating system used for critical and real-time applications where stability and reliability are of paramount importance.

On top of this core, Korg initially provided three software synthesizers. The first was a powerful sample and synthesis (S&S) engine based on a huge library of PCMs stored in ROM and on the OASYS's internal hard disk drive. Called HD-1, this engine was far more than an expanded Triton, and users could even determine its nature by loading expansion sample sets from the drive, as required. What's more, the sound quality of HD-1 was noticeably superior to other S&S workstations. The second synth (the AL-1) was a

superb virtual analog polysynth, while the third (the CX-3) was a remarkably accurate recreation of the Hammond organ. On top of all of this, Korg added the Wave Sequencing originally developed for its Wavestation synthesizer, vector synthesis, KARMA (a sophisticated cross between sequencing, arpeggiating and accompaniment software), a powerful sampler, MIDI sequencing, and a hard disk recording system. The response was immediate: the OASYS was critically lauded and it proved to be more popular than even Korg had expected.

Unlike previous instruments, whose capabilities (and limitations) were decided when their various VLSI chips were fabricated, the OASYS could remain a permanent work-in-progress, forever evolving to satisfy an enormous wish list that encompassed additional sound engines, more effects, improved sequencing and greater recording capabilities. Clearly, the company couldn't incorporate every possibility in the first version, but it wasn't long before the first upgrades appeared. In 2006, v1.1 included a "plucked string" synthesizer (STR-1) that was capable of much more than traditional string sounds. Next, Korg released expanded versions of two of its virtual analog synthesizers, the MS20EX and PolysixEX.

These proved to be very much more flexible and powerful than the same softsynths running on a conventional PC or Mac because they were fully integrated within the OASYS's audio environment, and thus able to take advantage of its sequencing, KARMA, and so on.

Most recently, Korg has upgraded the OASYS to version 1.3, adding an FM synthesizer (MOD-7) and further improving the KARMA software, and has also released a new sample library concentrating on brass and woodwind instruments.

At the time of writing, the OASYS remains at the forefront of keyboard design, combining almost everything that developers have learned over the past 100 years about keyboards and sound generation. How long it will remain there, or what will supersede it, are exciting questions yet to be answered.

keyboard facts

Using Keyboards

By Paul Ward

Like it or not, as a keyboard player you will usually be considered the geek of the band. As everyone else sees it, if you can handle all those knobs and buttons then you should certainly know how to fix the drummer's laptop computer, shouldn't you?

The truth is that getting a few sounds out of a typical home keyboard demands relatively little technical virtuosity. But replace the home keyboard with a semi-professional device, requiring external amplification, and the story begins to change rapidly. Add a second keyboard, MIDI, and mixing requirements and you're well on your way to geek status.

Using keyboards on stage, in a rehearsal room, or in a studio requires very similar considerations. Here I'll take a broad look at various aspects of the keyboard player's technical world that should help wherever you find yourself.

I'll also offer some techniques and tricks that I've learned over time. Some of the tips I'll pass on are as relevant in the digital, virtual instrument world as they were when an organ and electric piano were seen as the height of keyboard technology.

Choosing Keyboards

There is a vast choice of keyboards and sound modules out there, all of which have their merits and drawbacks. Inevitably there is a balance to be struck between cost, flexibility, portability, compatibility, functionality, connectivity, and other criteria that may be of critical importance to one player but of little or no interest to another. A player looking for a device to carry between bar gigs is likely to prefer portability over functionality, while a session musician will probably require a device that offers a wide, and easily accessible, palette of sounds.

It's clearly not possible to determine which keyboards or sound modules an individual should choose. If you long for a Mellotron and have the time, space, and patience to devote to it, then go for it. If, on the other hand, you are hoping to cut some funky beats on your laptop, a Mellotron might not be quite as suitable. As long as you take some time to think your needs through, and do a little homework, you will likely save yourself time, trouble, and money.

The most basic choice, when it comes down to synthesis technology, is between analog and digital.

Analog synthesizers have been with us for a long time, having their roots in some weird and wonderful inventions of the distant past, such as the "Singing Arc," the Ondes Martenot, and the Trautonium. Dr. Robert Moog's development of the "voltage control" system spawned the first synthesizers capable of realistically being used for live performance. Analog devices such as the Minimoog, the Prophet 5, and the Yamaha CS80 have a strong reputation for their warm sound (largely due to the vagaries of electronic circuitry) and programming immediacy (typically lots of one-per-function knobs and switches) while digital synthesizers are more precise and, arguably, feature more controllable functions. Clearly this is a vast over-simplification, and the difference is somewhat moot, but it will serve as a starting point.

For a while it seemed that analog was pretty much dead in the water, but constant waves of nostalgic interest have kept it alive to the point where new analog machines, for instance the Moog Little Phatty and the Prophet 08, are once again hitting the music stores. It's interesting to note that modern analog devices seem intent on rivaling digital technology's stability and control, while digital machines have been given the ability to add subjective "warmth" by emulating features such as analog oscillator tuning drift.

Modeling synthesizers, such as the Roland JP-8000 and the Novation Supernova, took the digital world a step further, effectively emulating many types of sound synthesis by "modeling" their characteristics in computer software. Although modeling techniques have largely been focused on mimicking analog synthesis, some manufacturers have also made reasonably successful stabs at modeling the physical characteristics of string, brass, and wind instruments, and even the human voice.

The next step in synthesizer technology is already in full swing, with virtual instruments (VIs) of all descriptions appearing on an almost daily basis. These, which include the Native Instruments Absynth, Rob Papen Albino, and G-Media M-Tron, are instruments that exist only in software, with no physical components. Typically they take the form of plug-ins within computer-based Digital Audio Workstation (DAW) software, such as Steinberg Cubase, Apple Logic, Cakewalk Sonar, and Digidesign Pro Tools. For some players a master keyboard and laptop computer may now be all they need. We'll take a closer look at VIs, their benefits and drawbacks, later. If you are planning to use a computer, then USB connectivity, or MIDI connectivity, should be high on the requirement list for your keyboard.

The instrument(s) you choose will depend on many factors, including familiarity, space, and the type of music you want to play. It's fair to say that some types of synthesizer are more prevalent in certain genres of music than others. The world of dance music, for example, still has a great love of analog synthesis. New ground continues to be broken with, in many cases, some very aging, though highly revered, instruments. Although it is often tempting to think that a certain type, or even model, of instrument is a prerequisite for producing a particular style of music, the truth is that anything goes—and your listeners are unlikely to know the difference.

Amplification

Ask 10 guitarists about their favorite amplifiers and speakers and it is almost certain that you will hear 10 significantly different opinions. Some are looking for warmth and distortion, others for a bright, cutting tone. What I doubt you will hear mentioned is "accuracy." A guitarist will choose an amplifier and speaker that give him a subjectively "good" sound with almost no regard for how subjectively clean, or "accurate" the result may be. I hasten to add that there's nothing wrong with this; the guitar, amp, and speaker essentially become one instrument in this context.

A typical modern keyboard is capable of generating myriad different sounds that stretch the entire breadth of the audio spectrum, from sub-sonic to super-sonic. For this reason most keyboard players will be looking for an amplifier/speaker setup that covers a wide frequency range and produces a subjectively neutral balance. For this reason, guitar amp/speaker "combos," usually favoring the mid-frequencies, are unlikely to suit a keyboard player.

There are, of course, areas in the world of keyboards where tonal accuracy is not only inappropriate, but positively avoided. A prime example would be the Leslie rotary speaker system, often employed for tonewheel organs, where the limited bandwidth, distortion, and notched frequency handling of the speaker becomes very much part of the instrument's character, in much the same way that a guitarist might pair a specific guitar and amp. Some keyboard players do, in fact, dedicate guitar combos to their lead synthesizer to share some of the tonal characteristics of a lead guitar, but it would be unlikely that the same setup would suit a piano or string sound. You can see that we are into highly specialized uses here.

Specific examples aside, a dedicated keyboard amp/speaker setup, for instance the Roland KC-550 or the Traynor K4, is usually a better choice, or even a small to medium PA system, if your budget can run to it. When playing live I have found the best policy is to send my keyboard outputs straight to the main front of house (FOH) mixing desk, rather than use an on-stage speaker system, though you could then push your own amp/speakers into service for on-stage monitoring. Sending the keyboards directly into the main mixer ensures that your sounds are getting to the audience unadulterated by the vagaries of microphones.

One approach might be to send a separate signal from each keyboard to FOH. With one or two keyboards this may be a reasonable option, though many players are, not without reason, nervous of entrusting their keyboard balance to someone else. Once you have a few keyboards or sound modules you will probably require a means of mixing together

the signals of those keyboards prior to sending the signal to FOH.

Some keyboard amplification systems come with an in-built mixer, but an external mixer is usually a preferred option, allowing for growth and upgrades in future. More importantly it allows the mixer to be placed close to the player, allowing for more flexibility during performance.

The choice of mixers is bewilderingly wide. At its most basic a mixer will include a number of mono and/or stereo input channels and a summed pair of stereo outputs. Many incorporate internal effects processors, sub-groups, cue/monitoring functions, and "scene memories" for storing mixes. How useful these features will be depends largely on the individual, but it would be fair to say that older keyboards are more likely to require the support of a more sophisticated mixer, since they often lack the effects, EQ, and patch memories (with which to store pre-set volume levels) of newer instruments.

Connections

There are two basic methods of transporting audio signals: analog and digital. Analog signals carry an electrical representation of the waveform, whereas digital signals carry a stream of binary data holding a digitized representation of the audio's waveform. These technologies are fundamentally different, as anyone who has accidentally plugged a digital output into an analog input will have found out very quickly.

First, let's take a look at analog signals.

In mainstream audio applications there are two major types of analog connection: balanced and unbalanced.

Unbalanced connections are very common on instruments such as keyboards and guitars, requiring a simple two-wire cable (usually a coaxial cable with a central signal wire surrounded by a shield connected to ground) to carry their signal. Typical connectors are quarter-inch TS (tip and sleeve) phone plugs (jackplugs). RCA connectors (phonos) are also used. The vast majority of professional and semi-professional keyboards will feature phone (jack) connectors.

Balanced audio connections are

most closely associated with microphone signals and rely on three pieces of wire to transport a signal from source to destination. Two wires carry a positive and negative version of the electrical signal and the third provides the ground connection. The beauty of a balanced connection is that it significantly reduces the effect of any noise picked up by the cable. How does it perform this piece of magic? The answer lies in those positive and negative signals. At the receiving end of a balanced connection the negative signal is flipped around to become positive. In doing so, any noise picked up on the cable's route becomes negated and cancels itself out:

Sent signal	= +signal / -signal
Received signal	= +signal + noise / -signal + noise
Processed signal	= +signal + noise / +signal − noise
Result	= +signal +signal

There are variations on this differential method, but the principle and overall aim remains the same: a hotter signal with less electrical interference. Balanced outputs on keyboards are something of a rarity, but it is usually wise to make use of them if they are provided. Balanced signals are most often provided on XLR or TRS (tip, ring, sleeve) phone/jack connectors. Don't confuse balanced connections with stereo connections; although they may use the same physical TRS connector they are fundamentally different in purpose.

It is a good idea to check the manuals that came with your keyboard and ensure you have the correct connectors and cables to make the best use of the available signals. A common mistake is to get balanced and unbalanced connections mixed up, which, though it may not do any real harm, means you are probably not making best use of the signal quality available to you. You also need to check that you are using the correct output levels to get the best signal-to-noise ratio from your signal chain. A good rule of thumb is to send the hottest signal you can (prior to the onset of distortion) from a keyboard, then reduce the signal, if necessary, in the receiving device. If you can keep the physical volume control on your keyboard at maximum this will help to achieve consistency when it comes to level-setting further down the signal chain.

Digital audio has two basic forms: electrical and optical. Electrical connections are usually found in the form of XLRs and RCA/phonos, whereas optical connections are set on a single standard most often referred to as TOSLINK (though, strictly speaking, this is actually the name of the connection system, as opposed to the type of connector). Digital cables can carry multiple channels of audio and can work at a variety of sample rates (most commonly 44.1kHz, 48kHz, 96kHz and 192 kHz) and word-lengths (most commonly 16-bit, 24-bit and 32-bit). The ADAT standard, for example, uses an optical cable to carry up to eight channels of 16-bit audio at a sample rate of up to 48kHz (higher rates/word-lengths can be carried with a reduction in the number of channels). Publications, blogs, and newsgroups are overflowing with arguments and counter-arguments over the relative merits of sample rates, word-lengths, filtering, dithering, and other digital considerations, but let's keep things simple here and say that, from the standpoint of general audio quality, the bigger the numbers, the better.

The two prevalent digital audio connection standards found in keyboards are AES/EBU and S/PDIF. An in-depth discussion of the two could fill a book of its own, but the good news is that, from a practical point of view, the differences are pretty much down to the type of physical connector: AES/EBU is most often found on an XLR and S/PDIF is usually in the form of an RCA (phono) socket. A simple XLR-to-RCA adapter is usually all that is needed to get the two conversing meaningfully with each other.

Digital audio connections would appear to offer a simple, noise-free solution. They are not prone to hum, hiss, and general interference in the same way as analog signal paths and their digitized nature means that there is no possibility of a difference in level-matching between items of equipment (though sample rates and word lengths need to be compatible). So what is the catch?

Unfortunately it is difficult to mix digital signals together. The reason for this is that all digital equipment needs a clock signal to be passed between source and recipient to ensure that data is sent and received at the correct time. Any mismatch in the timing between two pieces of equipment brings the potential for clicks, pops, dropouts, and other nasty artifacts in the resulting audio. Between any two devices this is not a problem, since a mutually agreeable clock signal can be established between them, and this is usually sent along with the digitized audio. But add a third device with its own independent clock signal and the recipient now has two, potentially conflicting, clocks to accommodate. The simplest way around this is to ensure that all the devices in a digital system work to a common clock source, which involves more cabling. This is probably fine in a studio environment, but for a typical keyboard rig it all starts to look rather fraught. No wonder that analog is currently still the connection of choice. If you only need to make a connection between a single keyboard and a digital mixer, however, it is probably worth investigating if it can be done digitally.

No matter what connection system you choose for your keyboards, I cannot stress highly enough that you should use good quality cables and connectors. I have seen otherwise enviable keyboard systems reduced to a buzzing mass of intermittent faults through the use of sub-standard cabling. A well-made, high quality cable will pay for itself over the years with better performance, lower noise, and higher resilience to damage. If you want to hear your equipment at its optimum then invest in the best. Use cable looms where possible to reduce the amount of clutter and, while you're at it, buy good keyboard stands.

Choosing keyboard sounds

There are whole books dedicated to the art of mixing. The art of achieving a subjectively "professional" mix from disparate musical elements, such as drums, guitars, bass, orchestras, and vocals, can be very rewarding. It can also be one of your most frustrating undertakings.

Keyboard players face some specific challenges, not least of which is that they can be called upon to play many musical roles. Within one piece of music, a player could be asked to provide a delicate piano introduction, add bass in the verse, conjure up a convincing orchestral string section in the chorus, double up some percussion, and then cut a screaming solo during the middle eight. Each of these sounds will require careful attention to tailor it to the needs of the overall mix.

When it comes to serving up the correct sound for a mix, bigger is not always better. Remember when you auditioned your spanking new synth in the shop? The lush, swirling pads, the chunky sequenced lines echoing around your head, and the patch that needed only one key press to sound like a symphony orchestra after a strong coffee break; impressive weren't they? Did you then try some of those patches in the rehearsal room, or in your busy mix? Didn't work as well there, did they?

Factory-loaded patches are there to sell an instrument in the shop. They are often multi-layered, over-fattened, swathed in copious amounts of effects and can pretty much constitute an entire mix on their own. Try to use them in the context of other instrumentation and you may find it difficult, because they need a lot of sonic space around them to work their magic, and that space is often not available. One option is to find a simpler patch, but you could also try thinning a factory patch out for yourself. Here's a quick list of patch-thinning techniques:

- Remove, or reduce, effects, particularly reverb and delays.
- Reduce the number of oscillators being used (particularly if they are playing octaves).
- Choose a simpler waveform.
- Apply some EQ or filtering to remove extreme highs or lows.
- Use some notch filtering to take out some mid-range clutter.
- Alter filter resonance.
- Play the part at a higher octave.

You could also try running patches through "stomp-box" effects pedals. I have a couple of electric piano patches that I regularly pass through a guitar distortion effect that reduces some low end and adds bite to the top to cut through a mix. In the studio I regularly run synthesizers through bench amplifiers (several of them the size of my palm), guitar amps, and pre-amplifiers, sometimes taking direct feeds and sometimes via a microphone. This removes some of the flab from a sound and adds a little random magic. It is surprising how often even the nastiest of sounds drops into a mix perfectly.

If you take a listen to some of the music you like most you will probably find the keyboard sounds are actually much simpler than a typical factory patch. When something truly gargantuan is called for then the supporting music needs to back off to make room for it. Think of your overall mix as if it were a play. If all the actors were standing at the front of the stage and shouting simultaneously the play would be a disaster. Choose whose speech is most important at any point in time and let them come forward to have their moment, moving the supporting cast back to allow room. If all else fails, ask yourself an important question: do I really need to be playing at this point in the song? Some of the most successful keyboard players understand when simply to take their hands off the keys.

The way a part is arranged makes an enormous difference to how it is perceived by a listener. A common failing of players adding orchestral parts to a mix, for example, is for them to play block chords, much as they would on an organ. Not everyone wants to study the finer details of orchestral arrangement merely to add a string pad to a rock ballad, but if you are striving to produce the illusion of a real string section a little appreciation of the basics will take you a long way and will be time well spent. If you are called upon to play convincing drum parts then it would be a good idea to envisage how a real drummer would play and emulate those characteristics, perhaps reducing the number of notes you are playing to allow for the limitations imposed by four overworked limbs as opposed to 10 busy fingers.

Having said all of the above, remember that there are no rules; if it works for you, then trust your ears.

There is one tip I'd like to leave you with above all else: learn to program your keyboards. Dig into

that manual, roll your sleeves up, and see what you can do. Make some sounds of your own: tweak, layer, stack, and detune patches. Be prepared to make mistakes and learn from them. You will have a lot of fun doing it and you'll begin to establish your own sonic signature, which is a defining mark of the most successful players around.

MIDI

In the days when audio was pretty much an exclusively analog art, the advent of MIDI brought with it a great deal of confusion. It is fair to say that in the digital world in which we now live that confusion has, if anything, increased. The main problem people seem to have with MIDI is that they fundamentally misunderstand the data that is traveling down a MIDI cable. This leads to a lot of misinformation and some very odd wiring systems.

This is not the place to discuss the lowest level intricacies of the MIDI protocol, so please forgive me if I gloss over that and give you one piece of vital information: MIDI is not audio. Please read those four words a few times and commit them to memory, because if you can recall them when you hit a MIDI-related problem it will help, I promise. And now I'd like to expand on those four words: MIDI is not digital audio either. So what is it?

MIDI is a communications protocol; in other words, a way for a device to send messages to another device. That message could say "open the curtains," "turn on the TV," or "switch on the light." These may seem like crazy examples, but they are actually quite possible. I'll admit that the curtain and TV examples are products of my imagination, but there really are stage lighting systems that utilize MIDI. What I am getting at is that MIDI is simply about messages.

Let's stick with the concept of an imaginary MIDI-equipped domestic lighting system for a moment. It has a MIDI input socket into which we have plugged a MIDI-equipped master keyboard. The keyboard is not capable of producing any sounds of its own: it is simply a MIDI controller. The lighting controller is designed to switch on a number of lights in our house, depending on which key is pressed on the

keyboard. The controller is set up so that when we press bottom C on the keyboard, the living room light comes on. When we release the key, the light switches off. So what messages have been sent between the keyboard and the lighting controller?

Pressing bottom C on the keyboard generates a MIDI message that tells the lighting controller that: a) an event has occurred; b) the event is a key having been pressed; c) the key that was pressed was bottom C. Now what? Assuming you are still holding your finger on the key, nothing happens, because no events are taking place. With no events to report, no messages are passed from the keyboard to the lighting controller, so the living room light remains switched on.

Eventually you lift your key from the keyboard and a message is generated from the keyboard to the lighting controller that says: a) an event has occurred; b) the event is a key having been released; c) the key that was released was bottom C. The lighting controller receives the message and switches off the living room light.

OK, let's unplug our keyboard's MIDI cable from the lighting controller (having found a lamp to see by) and instead plug it into a rack-mounted sound module.

Press that same bottom C key. What happens? Hopefully you'll have guessed that the keyboard sends out exactly the same message: a) an event has occurred; b) the event is a key having been pressed; c) the key that was pressed was bottom C. But what does the receiving sound module do when it receives this message? The honest answer is "it depends," but maybe we have a nice organ patch selected on the sound module and it plays an organ note of bottom C. Since you still have your finger on the key the organ note continues to sound indefinitely until you finally lift your finger and a message is sent to the sound module telling it that the key has been released.

Now you select a string patch from the sound module's front panel and play a bottom C on the keyboard again. The sound module now plays a string sound on bottom C. Notice that the keyboard is not telling the sound module anything about which actual sound to play; that decision is made by the sound module. In fact the keyboard is doing nothing but telling the outside world what your hands are doing on its keys. You could change the sound module to play any sound it is capable of, including drum sounds, but all the keyboard is saying is "play a bottom C." One recipient of the message played a musical note, but another switched on a light.

Hopefully you can now see why MIDI has nothing to do with audio. All MIDI does is report events and send messages; it has its roots in a computer communications protocol affectionately known as RS232. From our very simple example above you can now begin to see how other aspects of MIDI work. Missing from our example above is the concept of velocity, but this is actually very simple. The "note-on message" (which is really what we are generating by pressing a key) contains a value telling the receiving device how fast the key moved when it was pressed. It is up to the receiver to decide how to interpret the information; with higher velocity values the likelihood is that the played note would be louder, but it could just as easily open a filter, add vibrato, or play a different sound altogether.

Other events have their own message types. Modulation wheels, pitch wheels, foot and breath controllers, and patch selection buttons all have their own way of telling receiving devices that they have been activated, but it is always the decision of the receiver to decide what to do as a consequence.

With a basic grasp of MIDI under our belts we can now begin to broaden the picture. MIDI would be of limited use if all we could do was to join two pieces of equipment together. Adding more keyboards and sound devices to the MIDI chain is possible.

Let's add a third device to our imaginary keyboard and sound module setup. We will do this by taking a MIDI cable from the MIDI Thru socket of the sound module into the MIDI In of a sampler. Let's assume we have a few sounds loaded into the sampler's memory and we'll press that bottom C on the keyboard again.

This time we have two devices receiving the MIDI "note-on" messages from the keyboard. The message transmitted from the sound module's MIDI Thru port is simply a copy of the data being received at the module's MIDI In port. With our understanding of MIDI so far the conclusion might be that the sound module and the sampler would both play the bottom C in response to the message from the keyboard; and that would be a reasonable assumption to make were it not for the concept of MIDI channels.

MIDI channels can be likened to radio stations. A large number of radio stations might be transmitting at any moment in time, but your radio can only be "tuned in" to one channel at a time. MIDI has 16 channels available to it and a receiving device needs to choose one of those channels to "listen" to for its messages. Let's assume our MIDI keyboard is transmitting on channel 1. If both our sound module and sampler are set to receive messages on channel 1, then they will both play bottom C when that key is pressed on the master keyboard. But if the sampler is set to receive on channel 2 it will not play the note. By changing the transmitting channel of our keyboard we can now separately address up to 16 connected MIDI devices, but that's not all. How about if we "split" our keyboard so that notes below middle C transmit on channel 1 and those above transmit on channel 2? We can now play the sound module on the lower half of the keyboard and the sampler on the upper half. This split (or "zoning," since many key splits are in fact possible) facility is one of the basic functions of a master controller keyboard.

In the scenario above I mentioned the use of a MIDI Thru port. Thru ports are used to "daisy chain" a number of MIDI instruments together, allowing them to listen in on the MIDI data stream for anything that may be on their channel. It is quite possible to chain a large number of devices together using Thru ports, but this is not necessarily the best way to go about it. For one thing, the last device in the chain has a lot of reliance on the cables before it, so any problem with one connection would have an effect on every device further down the chain. Secondly, each time a MIDI signal is passed from a MIDI In to a MIDI Thru it goes through electrical (and/or optical) components. By doing so there is a slight degradation of the signal that can lead to data errors. In the early days of MIDI,

rumors abounded regarding MIDI timing delays caused by chaining devices in this way, but the truth is that any shift in timing was minimal (especially when considered alongside the time it takes some devices to process and respond to MIDI data); the potential for data errors is of greater significance, so if you are chaining more than four devices it is probably worth looking at a MIDI star network as an alternative.

Star networks are, as the name implies, based on a central transmission source with devices connected on a one-to-one basis with the central hub, like the rays from a star (or the spokes of a wheel). The advantage of this approach is that each device is seeing the data from the source, so there is none of the signal degradation associated with the daisy-chaining of devices using MIDI Thrus. Additionally, a breakdown, or error in transmission, on one of the spokes of the network does not affect the others, producing a more resilient system.

The hub of a star network is, in its simplest form, a MIDI Thru box, which takes a MIDI input and simply echoes it to a number of MIDI outputs. These devices are perfectly acceptable, but are rather hard to find these days. A more flexible solution is a MIDI patchbay, which offers patch memories but also sophisticated routing, re-channelizing (taking information sent on one MIDI channel and changing it to another), velocity scaling (which allows you to adjust your output to suit the weight of your touch on the keys), and other MIDI processing tools. Some computer MIDI interfaces can function as patchbays, whether or not they are connected to a computer, which makes them suitable for use in a MIDI-enabled studio and also for live performance.

One particularly useful feature of many MIDI patchbays (and some master keyboards too) is the ability to translate patch-change messages. In other words, you could, say, send patch 12 from your master keyboard and the patchbay would translate this into patch 2 on one sound module and patch 76 on another. This can sometimes get confusing, so it's a good idea to work through it slowly and make notes; but the result is a very flexible system that makes best use of patch-memory space and keeps the work you have to do at your master keyboard to a minimum. To some extent, USB has taken the place of MIDI as a connection to a computer and we will be taking a look at this.

Computers

In our example MIDI system so far we have a keyboard's MIDI out connected to a sound module's MIDI in and the sound module's MIDI thru connected to a sampler's MIDI in. This system is fine for live playing, but what about recording a performance?

We could, of course, simply record the audio by using microphones or taking the output from our devices (or more probably from our mixer) and plugging it into a recording device, such as a CD-recorder or a computer with appropriate recording hardware and software. There's nothing wrong with this approach if it gets the results, but it is very inflexible. Any error in performance is pretty much set in stone. If we decided later that we could have used better sounds—or played better—the performance would have to be replayed from scratch.

The answer is to record the MIDI event data that makes up the performance. As long as we capture all of the MIDI data that is transmitted by the player, and then reliably replay that data with the same timing nuances, we can effectively record and recreate the performance. After all, our sound module and sampler have no idea what is generating the MIDI data they are receiving and responding to. In this way we can now change patches and make other changes after the performance. We can also manipulate the MIDI data, perhaps changing velocity values, fixing wrong notes, or altering timing to correct or enhance a performance.

To record MIDI data we need some kind of storage and playback system. This can be in the form of a dedicated hardware MIDI recorder (or "sequencer," as they are often called), or a computer with suitable recording software. It is fair to say that computers are far more prevalent in this role, so that is where I will concentrate my attention here, but many of the same principles will apply to a hardware MIDI recorder.

So how does a computer fit into our imaginary rig? It will sit between our keyboard and our sound module/sampler. The computer now takes the MIDI data from the keyboard, records the data, and also passes it on to the sound module/sampler so that we can hear our performance.

To get MIDI in and out of a computer requires an interface. The most basic MIDI interfaces have one MIDI input port and one MIDI output port. The most you can do with this is address 16 MIDI channels. If the interface has two MIDI outputs you can address 32 MIDI channels. A dedicated MIDI interface is a useful tool for a player with multiple keyboard instruments. Many sound modules and keyboards are quite capable of responding on all 16 MIDI channels, so having them connected to dedicated MIDI output ports is very desirable; one device per MIDI port is a good way to go in those circumstances. An eight-in/eight-out MIDI interface may seem extravagant if you only have two keyboards and two sound modules, but if you can dedicate each to its own port you have an easier time of it.

Most MIDI interfaces use USB to connect to the host computer. It is worth checking the USB version of both the PC and the interface. Although it may appear to work, a mismatch of versions will result in data moving at the rate of the slowest device. Many MIDI interfaces will allow you to use them away from the computer, where they will act as a MIDI patchbay (and star network hub). This can be a great advantage.

Bringing MIDI data into a computer has the advantage of enabling us to redirect that data. In other words, we can decide where our MIDI data is coming from and where it is being sent. In our imaginary rig we can change the sending MIDI channel of our keyboard to address either the sound module on channel 1 or the sampler on channel 2. But imagine if we had 16 devices in our MIDI rig and we had to change the channel each time we wanted to play a different device. MIDI recording software "re-channelizes" incoming MIDI data, depending on which device is being addressed, meaning that we no longer have to change MIDI channel on our keyboard to address our sound module or sampler; the

computer and MIDI recording DAW software will now take care of this. This is one way that a computer and DAW can potentially be put to use in live performance, though there are more elegant solutions to MIDI routing for live use.

Many keyboards now feature USB ports for direct connection to a computer. In many ways this is a cleaner interface, and is a good solution for smaller setups, but USB ports tend to be in demand on computer systems and few USB-equipped keyboards offer more than one MIDI output for connecting further devices. Some keyboards require drivers to be installed to make use of their USB facilities, which can be problematical once you have two or more keyboards all wanting to join in the fun. The advantage of a MIDI interface is that, once its drivers are loaded and working, it will accept and handle any MIDI device you plug into it.

Whether you use a MIDI interface or a direct USB connection, the devices will show up in the computer's DAW environment as logical MIDI input and/or output devices. Some software allows you to give these devices friendly names, which is an option that can save a lot of time and head-scratching. Once assigned they will appear in drop-down lists as "Wavestation" or "Xpander," rather than the less helpful "Midex 8(2) 4."

It is worth taking some time to create a customized working environment in any piece of software, but with DAWs it can make a huge difference between an environment that works for you and one that puts up a fight each time you fire it up.

Once we have MIDI recorded into a DAW then we can manipulate it to get the performance we need. Maybe we can apply some quantization to tighten up the timing, move a few velocities to lift quieter notes, or transpose notes to change the feel of the part. MIDI is supremely malleable and it is worth taking time to make use of this fact until the performance is as you require it.

Ultimately your MIDI performance is required to be fixed as audio at some point. Some producers will take recorded audio (eg, vocals, guitars) and MIDI parts being played "live" and mix both sorts of sound down to an external audio recording device, such as a CD recorder or

keyboard facts

even analog tape. More likely a mix will be done "in the box," where the sound from both audio instruments and MIDI sound generators is recorded in its final form within the computer. Either way, I would suggest you always turn your MIDI parts into audio recordings prior to mixing. This allows for future mixes to be undertaken without your having to worry about whether the keyboard patches you used are still available. It also allows for some audio processing to be done in the DAW software, such as compression, EQ, or adding further effects that may not be available (or not be of the same quality) in the keyboard. To do this you will need to feed the audio from the MIDI-controlled keyboard and/or sound module into the computer/DAW via an audio interface. Then you run the track in real time while you record the audio signal. You can play back MIDI and record audio simultaneously on any DAW software. Make sure you have your MIDI volume at maximum to ensure the best signal-to-noise ratio.

Softsynths

Virtual instruments (VIs) or "softsynths," which are usually plug-ins for your DAW software, have exploded in popularity in recent times. Arguments rage over the merits of each, though the fiercest battles are reserved for VIs that purport to emulate "classic" hardware instruments of the past, such as ARPs, Moogs, Prophets, Hammonds, Mellotrons, and the like. Ultimately these arguments don't matter if you have an instrument that does the job.

There are a number of advantages to using VIs over hardware synths. They are reliable, requiring none of the maintenance and care that hardware demands, and there is no cabling to undertake to plumb a VI into your system. Since they exist only in software, a VI can be called up and used many times in a track, just as if you owned multiple pieces of hardware. For instance, if you are using a virtual Hammond organ (eg, Native Instruments' B-4), you can have one track of B-4 playing soft chords, another producing a distorted lead sound and yet another hitting some percussive chops for the rhythm. You are limited only by your

computer's processing capability. Your settings can be saved along with a track.

Many VIs can be controlled dynamically as a song plays, so you could have a filter opening and closing on the fly; although this can be done by hardware, achieving the same in software is considerably easier.

This all sounds very rosy, but there are disadvantages to VIs. Some can require a considerable amount of computing power to function, making them unwieldy to manage. DAW companies have realized this in recent years and have added dedicated "freeze" functions, enabling the sound of a VI to be captured and the VI switched off to free up the resources they would otherwise be using. This is a neat solution, but it adds some effort to a recording session and does little to help live performance. Although a VI will never suffer from the same reliability problems as hardware, including scratchy controls, dodgy cables and buzzing power supplies, a hardware instrument is not likely to be made obsolete by a computer's operating system upgrade.

Hardware keyboards and synths still have an edge when it comes to real-time manipulation, with dedicated application-specific controls, but you can buy hardware control surfaces that help VIs achieve similar results. Control surfaces come in a variety of forms, with buttons, knobs and faders in smaller or greater numbers. Connection is usually by USB or Firewire, so you will need to check that your computer has the relevant ports available. Although control surfaces are a great way to give hardware control to software, the fact that the layout and labeling of controls is, by necessity, generic, means that you still don't get the immediacy and friendliness of true, purpose-built hardware. Some controller systems have the ability to alter their labeling on the fly, usually in the form of LCDs above the controls, but these are still relatively expensive.

On balance, VIs are a boon to the creative player. Once the drawbacks are recognized, they can be mitigated and managed. It is fair to say that a combination of hardware and software is currently the optimum, but there are now a number of highly regarded and successful players

touring with little more than a master keyboard and a laptop computer.

To run a VI you need to have a computer of some description and this puts some players off using them for live performance. There are dedicated boxes that are able to run popular format VIs (typically VST instruments), but inside these are still computers. It has to be recognized that most modern keyboard/synth instruments are computers at heart in any case, though highly specialized ones, which makes them less susceptible to the vagaries of general-purpose computing platforms. That said, a typical computer brings a degree of flexibility that dedicated hardware cannot match. There are several software packages squarely aimed at live performance, enabling virtual keyboard racks to be assembled, effects installed and set lists to be constructed, all within a highly optimized environment. For players requiring transportability above all other considerations this is an appealing option. If entrusting the success (or otherwise) of your performance to a computer is an unsettling thought then hardware devices still hold their appeal.

If you do take the plunge to using a computer, then do yourself the biggest favor you can: back it up. By this I mean invest in some dedicated software that performs an image backup of your entire system hard drive. Make several backups, at least once every couple of months, save some at various physical locations and keep one with you at all times. Keep a history of backups and label them well.

The choice of softsynths is huge and getting bigger every day. Some are considerably costly, arriving with attendant hardware and sound libraries; others are produced under shareware licenses, or are even free, written by enthusiasts the world over. The most costly are not necessarily the best and the free ones are not always the worst. It is worth taking time to seek out the opinions of other users and to take advantage of demo versions before parting with money. There are some gems out there for little or no cost.

But please don't resort to piracy. If the people who program our software find they are getting a poor return on their work they will stop producing it: and it is we who will be the worst for that decision.

using keyboards

Preparing for live performance

A little planning goes a long way. It can make the difference between enjoying a performance and enduring it; feeling exhilarated by the experience, or wanting to run away and hide.

If we can take care of many of the technicalities before we reach the point of performance, we can make our lives a whole lot easier. For starters, how about rearranging our patches into some kind of order? It's all very well trying to remember that the brass patch for the second half of the fourth song is on patch number 58, but this starts to get tough when the number of patches to remember increases. How much easier might it be if we just stepped one patch along at every stage of the set and the correct patch was there waiting for us? Some keyboards even allow a "next patch" function to be assigned to a footswitch, so the player can keep his hands on the keyboard.

To hear some players speak, you would think that level setting was an arcane art on a parallel with the transformation of lead to gold. I have a simpler view of things. If you get your levels right in rehearsal, then they are pretty much the same levels you will need when you get to the performance.

The basic trick to getting your levels right is to work backwards from the patch requiring the most volume. By setting your mixer (keep the volume knob on all of your instruments set to maximum as far as possible) so that this patch can be heard in the mix you then have a starting point. Once you know that there is sufficient volume to handle the patch requiring the most volume, it stands to reason that there should be enough level to handle all of your other patches for the rest of the set. All that you now need to do is program your other patches to appropriate volume levels as you work through the set.

Rather than trust to the vagaries of some arbitrary "loudest" patch, in each of my keyboards and sound modules I program a "Soundcheck" patch that represents a 0dB reference output level from the device. In other words, when I play a bottom C on any device set to its "Soundcheck" patch I expect the mixer to register a level of 0dB on the input meters. This will be a very loud signal, so it's best to turn the mixer's outputs down before you set the 0dB level.

Once each device is set at 0dB using my "Soundcheck" patch I then run through each song in the set, adjusting the volume level of each patch on every device to give me a good balance. If I run out of steam for a particular patch I adjust the mixer levels for that device until I have an acceptable level, then I go back to my "Soundcheck" patch and reduce its programmed volume level to get it back to 0dB. If I do have to reset my "Soundcheck" patch level (which means I didn't set the initial mixer level correctly) I must then adjust any other patches I have made up to that point; the reason for this is usually that I didn't start out with the song requiring the most volume from the device. The first time you take this approach it may take a while to get the levels correct, but it comes easier with practice; remember that the patch requiring the most volume is very often the soft pad or the delicate piano. Some devices, particularly older keyboards, have no patch memories, but I get around this by either running them through a MIDI rack effect (which vintage keyboards tend to lack anyway), or using patch memories in a digital mixer.

So what is the result of all this effort? Once you get to the gig you now have simply to call up your "Soundcheck" patch on each device, play a bottom C and set the mix level of each device to 0dB on the mixer (or have the front of house engineer set it, if you do not use a mixer of your own). Once primed in this way you can be sure that all your relative patch levels are now ready to go for the entire gig. It's obviously difficult to legislate for the rest of the band tweaking their own levels as they go, but I have managed to convince the players I work with to use the same method with their own instruments and the result is a much more consistent mix and far shorter (and, in some cases, non-existent) soundcheck. In one band I played with we had all of the instruments connected to a MIDI-controlled mixer, controlled by a single master keyboard, so all of our levels and patch-changes were controlled by one player; the rest of us could all just get on with playing and forget about patch changes, effects and level settings for the entire set.

Many times I have been called at an inopportune moment to bail out a keyboard player in distress. Often this amounts to the loan of a device to replace one that failed during sound-check, but at other times the problem could have been avoided with a little planning. You would be amazed how many keyboard players I have met who carry no spare audio cables, then chant the "why me?" mantra when a cable fails just before the doors open.

I have a traveling case that I call my "overnight bag." This case contains a number of life-saving items. Here's a curtailed list of the contents: fuses, power cables, audio cables, MIDI cables, headphones, a selection of batteries (including some of those CR-xxx flat silver batteries, often found backing up the internal memory in hi-tech devices), multi-voltage power supply, memory cards, headphones, OS/data disks, gaffer tape, keyboard stand bolts, torch, MP3 player, portable hard drive, CD/DVD drive image backups, small mixer, cable tester, multi-meter, XLR "crossover" cables (usually with ground/return flipped), various plug/socket adapters.

Hopefully you will recognize that this collection of items is not, in any sense, a panacea; there are simply too many variables to anticipate every eventuality. But what it does do is anticipate the most obvious points of weakness and solve the problem before it happens.

No pliers, clippers, or soldering iron? At one time I did take these along to each gig, but over the years it became clear that a few ready-made leads are a better option. The last thing you need is to start a soldering session when you should be focusing on getting your whole rig into a working state as quickly as possible.

Hopefully most of the contents of my "overnight bag" are obvious candidates. The MP3 player is a useful diagnostic tool when audio doesn't seem to be getting where it should. I plug it into an audio cable and see if the music gets through; if not, then the problem is downstream of the player. The small mixer is a very simple mono six-channel device that would be far from ideal, but would suffice in an emergency.

But this isn't all. If your keyboard rig relies on some specific

keyboard facts

equipment it is good idea to play the "what if" game and fix the problem ahead of the event. I'll use the example of my Minimoog: I realized many years ago that if my Mini failed on me before a gig I would be pretty much stuck without my favored lead instrument. When I broke a fuse holder on the Mini the night before an important event, even though I managed to effect a repair, it did prompt me to take some positive action. Back in the rehearsal room I temporarily took the Mini out of my rig and worked through the set list without it. I set about making alternative patches on other devices to cover for the Mini and placing them on physical keyboards that made logistical sense. The process took some time and entailed several compromises, but the important thing was that I could now suffer the failure of a major part of my rig while still completing a set; far from ideal, but achievable nonetheless.

Over the years I have undertaken similar "what if" scenarios to work around the failure of various other key pieces of equipment and I have developed a system of patch numbering to help me out; if patch 1 on my master keyboard sets me up for the first number of the set, then patch 51 might be my contingency patch. Since all my devices set their patches from the master keyboard I have my entire rig ready to go with my alternative configuration. You can only go so far with this approach, but it pays to do what you can and I can honestly say I have always managed to get through a full set even when parts of my rig have given me trouble.

I keep a full set of data backups as far as possible, but there are some older data cards / disk types that are simply too hard to find these days. In these instances I will have identified alternative patches on other equipment during my "what if" sessions and have them under a contingency patch number, or even called up ready to go on a keyboard (or keyboard zone) that is otherwise unused at that point of the set.

Troubleshooting

I was once called in to simplify a keyboard rig that had grown into an unmanageable mess and involved its owner leaping from device to device, flipping patches, and pressing pedals

for all he was worth. His stage performances had become quite a feat of mental agility and physical dexterity, quite apart from the music he was playing. The whole rig had become a challenge, rather than a solution.

The first task was to begin to understand the devices making up the rig. There were several keyboards, each of which was assigned to control both its internal sounds and a number of attached sound modules. The player said that he often felt bound to purchase keyboards in preference to sound modules since, once a keyboard was placed in a MIDI chain, it was tied to producing sounds from that chain. He had little control of which modules produced sounds, short of leaning over to their volume controls to turn them down. Each keyboard, therefore, constituted the front end of a separate MIDI system. Some of the keyboards had MIDI sequencers built into them and these were used for part of the set.

This was clearly a rig that had grown organically. Each time a new device had been introduced it came in alongside the existing equipment. When attempts to integrate it into the existing rig had failed, it had been removed from the existing MIDI network and a new "mini-rig" had begun, which then began to sprout its own "offshoot" MIDI chain.

I first introduced the player to the time-honored technique of pen and paper. It is surprising how far a few pictures and words can go when working through problems. We mapped out all of the current connections, MIDI channels, controller inputs and audio routes. It was while doing this that we realized we could simply unplug a couple of cables that were actually doing nothing useful at all.

I had the player work through a few songs to see an example of the rig in action. Not only was the player switching patches on his keyboards, he was also changing them on the modules racked behind him. He said that the patch numbers in the keyboard and the attached sound module did not match up. For example, if he selected patch number 4 ("Piano") on the keyboard, then he wanted the sound module to produce a string sound to complement the piano, but the module had a guitar patch on number 4 and it was this sound that was being selected when

the sound module responded to the patch 4 MIDI command. To alleviate this, the sound module's patch reception had been switched off (so that it would now ignore any patch change command coming from the keyboard), but it now meant that patches had to be selected from the front panel of the sound module directly.

I decided to tackle this problem first. I switched patch reception back on in the sound modules and moved some of their patches into memory positions that did correspond with the keyboard's patch numbers. Now the keyboard and sound module patches were aligned. At certain parts in the song it was required for the sound module to change patch while the keyboard remained at its currently selected patch. To achieve this I simply duplicated the keyboard's patch to a new memory position and set up the sound module so that the keyboard's patch change selected a new sound from it, while calling up the same internal sound. I duplicated patches several times on the keyboard, because even though the keyboard was required to remain on one sound, the connected modules needed to be set to different patches as the song progressed and I wanted each change of "scene" to be the next patch along, rather than stepping forward and backward. This way, if the player was on patch 12, the next patch change would be patch 13, removing any doubt from the process. Although some keyboards allow "next patch" to be selected by foot pedal that was not the case here.

In this way we worked through a couple more songs and arrived at something altogether more workable, but it was also clear that we could do a lot more.

Firstly I used my 0dB patch leveling method to arrive at some relative mix levels for each patch. To solve the problem of switching a sound module on/off I created a "silent" patch that could be copied into patch positions where the module's contribution was not required. By running through a song and selecting patches on the keyboard the modules now called up the correct patch, at the correct mix level, and turned themselves down when not required.

I renamed keyboard patches to give us a clearer indication of use. "Piano 4" might be useful from a sound creation point of view, but "(Songtitle) Intro" and "(Songtitle) Mid8" are far more helpful on stage, and where we had reused the "Piano 4" patch in several songs the new name removed the potential confusion.

I had a much happier player with me by now, but there was still more we could do. I needed to establish a MIDI "star" network.

I installed a 16-in/16-out MIDI patchbay and to this we connected all the keyboards and each MIDI chain. At first I created a simple patch to ensure that everything functioned in exactly the same way as before I had added the patchbay. This gave us a starting point to build from. Now I separated each device from its MIDI chain as far as possible and gave each its own dedicated MIDI output from the patchbay. Again, I programmed up a "vanilla" patch on the MIDI patchbay that emulated things as they had been and tested this thoroughly.

Now we had our MIDI star network with the MIDI patchbay at its hub we could begin to make much better use of the rig. It quickly became apparent that some sound modules, duplicated by necessity in the old MIDI chains, could now be discarded, since one module could be shared between two or more keyboards. It was also now possible to assign sounds to a more convenient physical keyboard than had been the case previously.

The final step in simplifying this particular rig was to pass all of the patch-changing duties to the MIDI patchbay.

The patchbay we used was clever enough to understand when a patch change was required or not, i.e, it kept a log of which patch a device was currently on and if it knew the next patch change was the same patch, it did not send out a patch change message. This helped to reduce patch change "lag," where there is a moment of silence while a device loads up a new patch. Since the patchbay now took care of the connected devices we could reduce the amount of patch duplication and add some MIDI volume commands to set devices up for each part of the set, further reducing the number of separate patches required.

The result of all this effort was a slicker, slimmer, more capable keyboard rig, and one considerably happier keyboard player. This is quite

an extreme example, but it does highlight the importance of understanding a problem, adequately familiarizing yourself with the tools at your disposal and then making the link between the two (it will probably come as no surprise that the keyboard player above not only had never read many of the manuals for his devices, he actually couldn't find most of them). The same principles apply equally to the world of virtual keyboard-based environments. The careful creation of virtual MIDI "racks," patch placement, patch-naming, and sequential patch selection is equally relevant and pays back dividends if carefully applied.

Conclusion

Modern electronic keyboards are little short of technical miracles. Even home keyboards contain technology that a short time ago would have astounded professional players surrounded by electronic keyboard wizardry.

The advent of physical modeling and virtual instruments is taking us into a world where anything is possible, unbounded by the physical requirements of electronic components or moving air. We are truly arriving at a time when, if an instrument can be imagined, then it can probably be designed in software.

But our interface with the new world of instruments has its roots in the past. For reasons of practicality, familiarity, and general acceptance, new instruments are built to offer a similar interface to instruments of the past. MIDI is still very much with us, having survived the transition to USB and Firewire connections, and we still talk of oscillators, filters and envelopes, whether they be generated by electronics or software.

Hopefully some of the information I've given you here will help to understand the application of the new technology available to you and inspire you to go further. There are plenty of sources for more in-depth information and I'd advise you to seek them out. The more knowledge you have about your keyboards then the better placed you will be to take advantage of their power and the sheer exhilaration they offer when you are able to master that power to perform the music you love.

Synthesizer Basics
By Steve Lodder

In the early 70s, three instruments radically simplified the process of synthesizing sound, making it a practical possibility for the working musician. The Minimoog, with its limited but flexible control panel, led the way in accessibility; the ARP 2600 featured a hard-wired setup that could be over-ridden with patch-cords; and EMS settled on a pin matrix system for the Synthi AKS, its entry into the commercial market. A system began to emerge for organizing the building blocks of synthesis into a transportable unit. That basic organizational framework has survived the ups and downs of the music technology market, the arrival of software synths, and the development of virtual analog systems. It survives because the elements are easy enough to understand, but flexible enough to be interesting and inspiring.

At the most basic level, you need an oscillator to initiate the noise, a filter to change its timbre, and an amplifier, coupled with an envelope generator and a keyboard, to say when the noise starts and how long it lasts. In the designs of the 1970s, the flow of audio signal from one element to the next would follow the path shown in the diagram.

Looking from left to right, the term VCO refers to a Voltage Controlled Oscillator. That "Voltage Controlled" means that the frequency and character of the oscillator's output is determined by control voltages from elsewhere in the synthesizer: from the keyboard, the control panel, or another oscillator. In the diagram, as in a Minimoog, there are two VCOs plus one LFO, a Low Frequency Oscillator. The LFO can be used for making noises, but is more likely to be used to transform other parameters.

For each oscillator there is a choice of waveform; sine waves, square waves, sawtooth, and pulse waveforms are common options. Each waveform has its own sonic characteristic; some are richer in overtones or upper harmonics, some are smoother. The sine wave is closest to an uncolored fundamental tone; its sound can be compared to a softly blown flute. The square and sawtooth

keyboard facts

waves contain harmonics that add upper color to the sound. The square wave generates odd harmonics only, i.e., the third, fifth, etc, which translates into a hollow, reedy quality. The sawtooth is the richest sound, as it contains an even spread of harmonics; it can be equated with a brass sound. The pulse waveform is useful for imitating string sounds.

The audio signal from the oscillators is combined in the mixer, before being routed to the next stage. Sometimes there's an option of adding white noise into the mix. It contains all frequencies at an equal level, and is very good for roughing up the sound or for Star Wars effects.

The next stage is the VCF (Voltage Controlled Filter), which tends to come

As part of the filter section, the resonance control, also known as "Q" or filter emphasis, plays a part in shaping the sound. Used in subtle ways, the resonance control emphasizes frequencies either side of the frequency to which its cutoff control is set, in the same way that the resonant box of an instrument such as the violin accentuates the frequencies of the strings. Used in more extreme ways, the filter squeaks and bleeps, and clicks arise when the resonance is set so high that the filter starts to self-oscillate. If it is set right you can even play these sounds as a pitch.

The final stage, the VCA (Voltage Controlled Amplifier) not only dictates the final audio level, it determines what happens when a key is pressed,

It can be patched to another oscillator to "modulate" its output. In other words, it supplies an oscillating control voltage that can alter the pitch of one of the VCOs. If the LFO's waveform is set to a sine wave, it will make the VCO's pitch move gently up and down, producing vibrato. If it is set to sawtooth, the pitch will rise gently and drop rapidly, producing a harsher "nee-naw" effect. You can also use the LFO's oscillating voltage to control the cutoff of a filter, making the timbre of the sound change. And if you apply the LFO's voltage to the VCA you can have a tremolo effect.

The possibilities of an analog setup are endless—or "limited only by your imagination," as the manufacturers say—because the routing of the component modules to one another can be very complex indeed. You can apply an envelope to a filter or the waveform of an oscillator; you can use the velocity of the keyboard to control a filter's cutoff; and so on. Combining hard-wired circuits with patch-cord modulation applied to multiple destinations can cause havoc—creative havoc—to an oscillator trying to behave in a stable manner.

Thanks to Bob Moog, Alan Pearlman at ARP, and David Cockerell at EMS, the synthesizer became a player's instrument, rather than an educational programmer's tool.

Now imagine a world without VCOs, where instead of having oscillators as your starting point, your building blocks are audio recordings, digitally preserved in the memory of your keyboard. That's roughly where we are today; from home low-end keyboards to high-end synthesizer workstations, the sound is sourced from ROM wave memory. This means that instead of "synthesizing" a guitar sound, what you are doing is playing back a recording of a guitar, in exactly the same way as a sampler does. The usual filter and envelope controls are still available, and if you want to synthesize from scratch, most synths include a chunk of the basic saw, sine, square, and so on in their waveform list. However, if you want to truly synthesize in the digital age, you'll have to look for a physical modeling structure, where the synth/computer actually mimics the behavior of an analog circuit, or blown pipe, or bowed string. That's a whole other ball game.

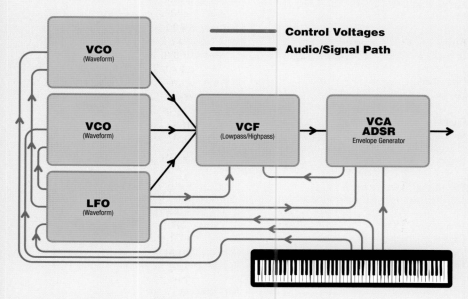

Control Voltages
Audio/Signal Path

in two types: low-pass and high-pass. The most common is the lowpass filter. It lets through all the frequencies when fully open, but progressively blocks the higher frequencies as it is closed down. If you were to play a high note on the keyboard, setting the VCF to "off" would probably extinguish the fundamental as well as the upper tones, resulting in silence. Mostly though, the VCF is used to make fine adjustments to the presence of upper harmonics: i.e., how much top/brightness there is to the sound. In that way a detailed, bright string patch can become a smooth distant pad at the turn of a knob. Not surprising then, that every self-respecting synth has a way of grabbing this parameter easily and quickly.

held down, and released. Its envelope generator shapes the sound in time. ADSR stands for the parameters you can adjust in the envelope generator: Attack, Decay, Sustain, and Release. Attack controls how long it takes for the sound to reach its full level when the key is pressed. Decay controls how long it takes for the sound to drop to the Sustain level. Sustain is the level the sound maintains until the key is released. Release determines how long the sound continues once the key is released. Early synthesizers did not always allow the adjustment of all the parameters of the sound envelope: some just had ADS or ADR envelopes. A second envelope generator was also common.

The LFO can produce sounds, as we have seen, but it has another use.

Action
The mechanism by which a piano makes a sound.

Additive synthesis
System in which waveforms tuned to different harmonics are combined.

ADSR (Attack, Decay, Sustain, Release)
Part of a synthesizer that controls the loudness of its sound over time.

Aftertouch
A MIDI control signal that generates a message based on the pressure exerted on a key.

Amplifier
Electronic circuit that increases the level of a signal.

Analog (UK: analogue)
Relating to signals created by a continuously variable voltage; as opposed to digital.

Arpeggiator
Device or setting for creating automatic arpeggios.

Arpeggio
Playing the notes of a chord one at a time.

Attack
Speed at which a sound reaches its maximum level.

Audio interface
A device that routes audio into and out of a computer.

Balanced
Signals or in/out connections where a pair of conductors (hot and cold) are separate from the ground (earth) shield. Avoids noise problems and permits longer cable runs than unbalanced working.

Barrelhouse
Piano style of the early 20th century.

Bebop
Type of jazz originating in the 40s and notable for its complex harmonies and rhythms.

Bit depth
The number of bits used to represent a single sample in an audio file.

Channel
(1) Path through which signal passes.
(2) Path for MIDI data.

Check
Mechanism that prevents a piano hammer from bouncing back and striking the string more than once.

Clock speed
Speed at which a computer processes information.

Combo
Amplifier and loudspeaker in the same box.

'Comping
Accompanying a solo in jazz.

Compression
Reducing the dynamic range of an audio signal.

Compressor
Hardware or software system for compression.

Controller
Device used to send MIDI messages, for instance a MIDI keyboard.

Control surface
Mixer-like device that provides physical control of a software instrument.

Damping
System that cuts off the sound of piano strings when a key is released.

DAW (Digital Audio Workstation)
Hardware device or computer software that permits audio and MIDI recording, editing, and mixing.

Decay
Gradual drop in level of a sound or signal.

Decibel (dB)
Unit for measuring audio levels.

Digital
Relating to signals that are created from a series of numbers (binary 1s and 0s); as opposed to analog.

DSP (Digital Signal Processor)
A device used to process digital audio.

Duophonic
Capable of playing two notes at once.

Effect (Also FX)
Term for audio processing such as distortion, delay, reverberation, and so on.

Envelope generator
Part of a synthesizer that controls the loudness of the sound over time.

Equalization (EQ)
Tone control.

Escapement
Part of piano action that allows the string to continue to vibrate after it has been struck.

Event
Any MIDI occurrence or change, such as hitting or releasing a controller key.

Filter
Electronic device or circuit that allows only certain frequencies to pass.

Firewire
Interface for connecting peripherals to a computer.

FM (Frequency Modulation)
Type of digital synthesis.

Gain
Amount of increase of signal level. When dBs are used, increased gain is shown as +dB; reduction is –dB; no change is 0dB.

Gliss (Glissando)
A glide from one pitch to another.

Harmonic
An overtone created at the same time as the fundamental tone of an instrument.

Hub
Device that allows you to expand the number of connections in your system.

Input
A connection that allows signal or control information to enter a system.

Interface
A device that routes signal to or from a computer, either a MIDI interface or an audio interface.

Jack (UK: jack socket)
Mono or stereo connecting socket, usually quarter-inch.

Leslie
Speaker system using revolving horns, usually coupled with the Hammond organ.

LFO (Low-Frequency Oscillator)
Synthesizer component that creates pulsating rhythms rather than audio tones.

Loop
(1) v. To repeat.
(2) n. Section of audio or MIDI that repeats.

Manual
One keyboard on a multi-keyboard instrument, for instance an organ.

MIDI interface
Device for connecting MIDI instruments to a computer.

MIDI (Musical Instrument Digital Interface)
Industry-standard system for transmitting and receiving notes in electronic instruments and computers.

Mix
(1) v. To combine multiple audio signals for output.
(2) n. The combined audio recording that results.

Mixer
Device for collecting, processing, and combining audio signals.

Modeling
Technology that allows digital instruments to emulate analog synthesizers or acoustic instruments.

Modulation
Audio effect that uses delay and pitch to alter a sound over time.

keyboard facts

Modulation wheel
Control on keyboard that adjusts modulation effects.

Multitrack
A device capable of recording and playing back multiple tracks of audio.

Note
In MIDI, a message that triggers a sound in a MIDI device.

Oscillator
An electronic device or circuit that produces a fluctuating signal, often a sound.

Pad
A synthesizer sound used for background harmony and atmosphere.

Pan
Control that positions a sound in a stereo field.

Parameter
Any aspect of a sound or device that can be controlled.

Patch
(1) n. A combination of settings (for instance in a synthesizer) that can be stored for later use.
(2) v. To connect devices together.

Patchbay
Device used to set up patches.

Patch cord
Cable used to create patches.

PCM (Pulse Code Modulation)
Standard method for encoding audio samples.

Pitch bend
(1) MIDI message that alters the pitch of a note.
(2) Keyboard control that alters the pitch of a note.

Plug-in
Software that adds capabilities to a system. Includes effects processors and software instruments.

Polyphonic
Of synthesizers, capable of playing several notes simultaneously.

RAM (Random Access Memory)
Computer memory.

Reed
Flat metal vibrating element used in some electric pianos.

Release
The amount of time taken for a note to fade after a key is released.

Reverb (Reverberation)
Ambience effect combining many short echoes.

Riff
A repeated melodic or rhythmic figure.

Root
The note in a chord or scale that gives it its name.

Sample
(1) The smallest unit in a digital audio recording.
(2) An audio recording that can be triggered by a sampler.

S & S (Sample and Synthesis)
Digital synthesizer technique that combines samples with generated sounds.

Sampler
A device that can record and play back audio samples at different pitches.

Semitone
A half-step between notes; the smallest interval in Western music.

Sequencer
A device or software program that stores and plays back MIDI information.

Signal processor
A device that alters a signal, particularly for audio effects.

Soft synth
A synthesizer that exists only as software.

Software instrument
A software emulation of a physical instrument.

Split
To set up a synthesizer keyboard so that different physical regions play different sounds.

Standard
A tune or song of established popularity.

Star network
System for connecting several MIDI devices to a central hub.

Stop
Tone control on organ and some early pianos.

Stride
Semi-improvised piano style of the early 20th century.

Sustain
Length of time a note is held for.

Synchronize
To lock two devices together so they play back together.

Syncopation
Displacement of the normal beat.

Synthesizer
Electronic instrument used for sound creation, using analog or digital techniques.

Tempo
Speed of a musical passage.

Thru
MIDI connection that passes information through one device to another.

Timbre
Tone quality of a sound.

Time code
Synchronization information.

Tine
Vibrating element in a Fender Rhodes piano.

Tonewheel
System of generating sounds used in the Hammond organ.

Track
A channel of audio or MIDI information.

Transpose
To change pitch or key of a musical passage or audio track.

Tremolo
Rhythmic fluctuation of volume.

Unbalanced
Cables and connectors using a single signal wire and a surrounding shield.

USB (Universal Serial Bus)
Interface for connecting peripherals to a computer.

VCA (Voltage Controlled Amplifier)
Envelope generator which controls the loudness of a sound over time.

VCF (Voltage Controlled Filter)
A filter whose parameters are controlled by altering applied voltages.

VCO (Voltage Controlled Oscillator)
An oscillator whose frequency is controlled by an applied voltage.

Velocity
A MIDI parameter that measures the force with which a key is struck.

Vibrato
Rhythmic fluctuation of pitch.

Virtual instrument
A synthesizer existing only as software.

Voice
Each of the sounds capable of being produced simultaneously by an electronic instrument.

Voltage control
A system for controlling another circuit (for instance, an oscillator or an envelope generator) by altering a voltage.

Waveform
A curve showing the shape of a wave at any given time.

XLR
Three-pin audio connector.

96 acknowledgments

TOTALLY INTERACTIVE
KEYBOARD BIBLE
Tutor Book, Keyboard Facts, DVD, CD

The publishers would like to thank the following for their contributions to this project.

Keyboard Facts

Gordon Reid; Paul Ward; Carl Humphries; Thomas Jerome Seabrook; Mark Brend; John Morrish; Steve Lodder; Peter Chrisp; Tony Bacon; Jon "Mojo" Mills. Artist pictures supplied by Redferns Picture Library, London. Instrument pictures from the Balafon Image Bank, except Mellotron, p.68, supplied by Gary Knight. Picture of Clara Schumann, p.49, from the Lebrecht Collection.

DVD

Steve Lodder; Janette Mason; Colin Mottram and Kathy Plaskitt of Lenzflare. Instruments supplied by Terminal Studios of London. DVD shot at Battersea Arts Centre, London.

Tutor Book

Steve Lodder; Janette Mason; Carl Humphries.

CD

Steve Lodder; Janette Mason.

Design

Paul Cooper Design; Johnathan Elliott of Mental Block Design & Marketing; Balley Design Associates.